SHARE YOUR JOY

MIXED MEDIA SHAREABLE ART

Sarah J. Gardner

Quarto.com • WalterFoster.com

© 2023 Quarto Publishing Group USA Inc.
Artwork & text © 2023 Sarah J Gardner

First published in 2023 by Walter Foster Publishing, an imprint of The Quarto Group.
100 Cummings Center, Suite 265D, Beverly, MA 01915, USA.
T (978) 282-9590 F (978) 283-2742

Walter Foster Publishing titles are also available at discount for retail, wholesale, promotional, and bulk purchase. For details, contact the Special Sales Manager by email at specialsales@quarto.com or by mail at The Quarto Group, Attn: Special Sales Manager, 100 Cummings Center, Suite 265D, Beverly, MA 01915, USA.

27 26 25 24 23   2 3 4 5

ISBN: 978-0-7603-8309-4

Digital edition published in 2023
eISBN: 978-0-7603-8310-0

Library of Congress Cataloging-in-Publication Data available

Printed in the United States

Contents

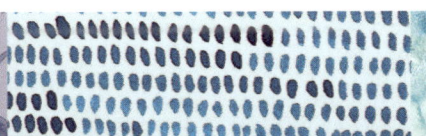

Introduction

Welcome to the joyful world of shareable art! Making art to share—to give away—is a great way to begin your exploration of mixed-media art. It's how I started my creative journey. Whether you're a beginner or a mixed-media maven, when you share what you create, you're sharing the joy that you experienced making it.

This book is an introduction to my style of mixed-media art as I learned to create it—by making art to share. From postcards to artist trading cards to mini journals and zines, I have been making art and sharing it for many years. This book contains much of the knowledge and experience I have accumulated thus far in my creative journey.

I hope this book will inspire you. Whether you're using it to get started on your mixed-media journey or as part of your ongoing creative practice, I encourage you to get curious and pay attention to what excites *you*.

Creating is where I give myself permission to play.

This journey has been so joyful for me! Shareable art is a way to spread that joy to others. Teaching about the creative process that brings me joy is another way to do this—and so is this book. As you create the art papers and the shareable projects here, I hope you experience the joy of creating mixed-media art to share and that, when you share it, you'll bring joy to someone else.

Allow me to introduce myself. I'm Sarah J. Gardner, also known as Juicy*S. I live with my family in

a small surf town called Cardiff-by-the-Sea in Southern California. I'm a practicing lawyer, a cancer (tongue) survivor, and a self-taught mixed-media artist and teacher.

Juicy*S is my DJ name. I'm not a DJ. I would love to be a DJ. It's one of my dream jobs! I started my first art blog in 2009 with this name, and I've had it ever since.

I'm the girl (yes, even though I'm fifty-something, I'm still a girl!) who has a tutu dance party and makes every one of her guests their own tutu. What can I say?! I really like to make things! Even though I'm a fierce multitasker, I make an effort every day to notice the miraculous in the mundane. I love the way the Pacific Ocean sparkles in the wintertime, the softness of my dog Ulu's ears, and the inside of that security envelope (that came in the mail with a bill!) I know I can transform into an art paper!

Perfection isn't the motivating force.

Creating is where I give myself permission to play, experiment, learn, and enjoy the process. I've learned a lot over the years about different art supplies, or media, and what they do, what I like and don't like, and how colors work together. I get joy out of the process of creating something that I think is beautiful.

In the past, I sometimes had difficulty making time for myself and for creativity. Over time, I realized that I *needed* to spend time this way to be happy and productive, as well as supportive to others in my life.

I think it finally hit me in 2021 when I did The 100 Day Project: I can make something just for the pure joy of making it. I can do this every day. I can leave art supplies and works in progress all over my house! I don't have to justify it in my own mind, and I don't have to explain it to anyone else!

I did clean up after finishing The 100 Day Project, though. I made 100 paper mobiles in 100 days. The main takeaway from it was that I don't use having to clean up as a reason *not* to make a mess anymore!

I'm also the kind of person who thinks a lot (maybe too much) about things. I'm a recovering perfectionist. Through all the years I've been making stuff, I've learned that what gives me joy is the *process* of creating, not the "perfect" end result. I still want things to turn out in a way that I like, but perfection isn't the motivating force or the unkind dictator in my head anymore.

When I'm creating, I'm really focused on the process, enjoying the intuitive way things happen, seeing what different supplies do, and experimenting and playing around without judging every choice I make. I'm indulging my curiosity and open to what can happen, even mistakes and messes. Sometimes these turn out to be the best part! I'm not thinking about a result; I'm not in production mode. I'm in the moment, attending to the different choices I make along the way, with each choice leading to another and another. I feel a sense of flow, of being "in

the zone." I lose track of time and feel connected to myself because I am fully and intentionally engaged in the transformative process of creating something new out of my supplies.

Attitude and mindset while creating keep me in the moment.

When I get out of my own way like this, I feel more like a whole person. Staying curious and being kind to myself, trusting this process, can be a meditation. I can experience joy, awe, and wonder. I see that everything turns out, even if I don't follow a plan or end up with something perfect. I learn that the attitude and mindset I have while I'm creating is an attitude and mindset that will keep me in the moment and allow me to experience joy, even in the daily chores that need to be done.

Creativity Can Be Self-Care

Quite often, I hear people say, "I wish I were creative like you!" I always tell them, "You *are* creative!" You may tell yourself you are not creative, but that's your inner critic talking. The perfectionist in me would keep me from trying, learning, and growing if I let it. But I know now that you can't do anything until you learn how to do it! Learning means making mistakes and practicing. If you're just starting out, you may have a little frustration because what you are making isn't matching up with what you envision. You have to work through this. Find what you like. Take what you like and make it your own. Do this with a lot of things, and over time, your work will start to become something you like. All the while you will be experiencing the joy of creativity.

Mindfulness is being attentive to what's happening now. Our assumptions (about ourselves, our ability, or what's good or bad) and our limiting thoughts are all part of our history—they are grounded in the past. Our worry and fear of not being good enough, or failing, is about the unknown—the future. What's left is something in between—the present moment. This is where we bring our attention as we create. I believe that creativity is mindfulness in action.

Let's sling some paint and share some art.

Let's take in what's happening now and ask, "What if?" Instead of judging, let's just be playful, waste paint, and scribble like a kid.

Creativity is my self-care. I want to help others who may think too much or who want to explore creativity to get out of their heads, ignore that perfectionistic inner critic, and play around with art supplies. It gives me joy, and I want to share this way to happiness. This is my wish for you. What's your DJ name? Let's sling some paint and share some art, and you can tell me all about it!

Camps, Community, Connection

Every summer, I hosted Girls' ARTisan Camps at my home for my daughter and her friends. I'd set up all the supplies and "table settings" on the front deck. These camps were a bonding experience for all of us. We explored mixed-media art: bookbinding, art journaling, embroidery, garment dying, mandala coloring, papier-mâché bowl-making, paper lanterns, paper mobiles, paper prayer flag-making, and beyond. It was about making a mess, making beautiful mistakes, and just being playful. And of course, we'd make a lot of art to share: postcards, greeting cards, and journals.

Making art with your friends is fun! But the girls would also explore their inner worlds with art journaling and deep conversations. These camps

were about more than just art lessons. They were a place for connection, to self and to each other; they were about life lessons.

When the parents came to pick up the girls after camp, they'd always say, "I wanna do art camp!" No kidding! The girls would play with paint and spray inks, dribble liquid acrylic, sponge through stencils, and journal about what makes them amazing humans!

Once the girls were grown and I stopped doing the camps, I missed this dedicated time for creativity and thought, why not do art camp for moms like me? That's how the Juicy*S Art Play Date came to be. My Art Play Dates give us a chance to feel free to play with art supplies in a

fun, supportive gathering with like-minded others. I host these on the deck and in the backyard, just like the Girls' ARTisan Camps!

We are so entrenched in our adulthood that we may be uncomfortable just letting ourselves be playful, curious, and unafraid to make a mess. If we adopt an attitude of playfulness, we free ourselves from the adult in our head who tells us we are too old for this.

I hope that you will experience *Share Your Joy* as an art camp (or an Art Play Date) in book form! Approach it with a childlike attitude of playfulness and curiosity if you're an adult. If you're a kid, just be yourself!

My Mixed-Media Mantra

One of the truths that came out of many years of making art with kids is this: Anyone can do this! Mixed media, for me, is about asking, "What if?" It is about surrendering to the process so you can be in the moment; it is not about creating a "perfect result" or a "work of art." Like the girls concluded, your art is special just because it is *your* art. And it's yours because of the process you engaged in to create it. My process, as I've said, is to make choices along the way and use each choice to make the next one. When I do this, I'm not following a plan. I'm just making one choice after the other. I layer different media, creating a push and pull between darker layers and lighter

ones. I play with color, layering that too. My mixed-media mantra is "Layer till you like it!" If I don't like it, it's not done yet.

Using this book, I hope you will explore what you like in making the art papers and the shareable projects I've created for you. It can be a process of trial and error. Embrace this process because there is much to learn from it. Attending to the choices you make and the outcomes of those choices will help you discover what you like and don't like. It's a little bit like life. If you fully invest yourself in this process of discovery, you will end up loving, not just liking, what you create. And that love . . . that is the "joy" in *Share Your Joy*.

Mixed-Media Toy Box

For me, mixed-media art is all about playfulness. It's an opportunity to have fun, make a mess, experiment with what art supplies do, and embrace the unexpected. It's more like playing with toys than working with tools! (So I couldn't call it a "tool box," right?)

Choosing a Limited Color Palette

Creating is always easier when you aren't overwhelmed with color choices and you know where to begin. I like to choose a limited color palette at the beginning to get myself excited about what I will create. Then I have all the paints I am using at the ready, and whatever I make has a cohesive color scheme.

To make choosing a color palette easier, I created a swatch ring of all my acrylic paints. Then I use this big ring to select swatches for a limited color palette and create a smaller swatch ring to use while I'm creating. The top right photo on this page shows the small swatch ring for all the art I created for this book. You can watch a short video demonstrating this by scanning the QR code to the right.

Substrates: For the purposes of this book and the projects you'll create, "substrates" means "paper." In general, a substrate is the surface you're working on. You apply media—like paint, mark-makers, and watercolor—to a substrate to create a piece of art. I create mixed-media mail art out of a lot of different papers. I create art papers out of some of these, and I apply the art papers and other collage materials to more substantial ones. Pictured below, from left to right, are watercolor paper, scrapbooking card stock, Bristol (heavy card stock), brown packaging paper, light watercolor paper, newsprint, sketchbook paper, printed scrapbooking papers (3), sheet music, vintage ledger paper, book text (2), a security envelope, and precut and folded note cards. Not pictured is sulfite paper, a very inexpensive kind of light construction paper. It holds wet media pretty well but is thin enough to be great for collage, so I love to use it for art papers.

Adhesives: I use various brands of glue sticks interchangeably. Fluid matte medium works best for collaging tissue paper, decorative napkins, or deli paper art papers as the fluidity helps them meld better into the artwork. I use soft gel matte medium in my mixed-media layers to adhere most other collage materials. Two-sided tape comes in handy for certain applications, as you'll see! I use a product called Art Glitter Glue because it is a fast-drying glue with a precision applicator that works really well for gluing small items.

Gessos and grounds: I use matte varnish to coat other media, like shiny acrylics or oil/soft pastels. That way, I can write or doodle onto the surface in my finishing stages. I use clear gesso to create a "tooth" on my surface so that other media will go down better.

White gesso is a mixed media must-have. Normally, it's used to prepare canvases or other surfaces so that paint goes on more easily and with less waste. But mixed-media artists use gesso for all kinds of things. Mainly, I use it in creating the layers I love. I apply it over vibrant color to add interest, contrast, and more depth. I use it for stenciling instead of white paint. It has a rough, matte surface, which I often need for final doodling layers in my work. Absorbent ground is like gesso, but it is not as opaque. I like to use this to add a sheer, cloudy layer over book text before adding watercolor.

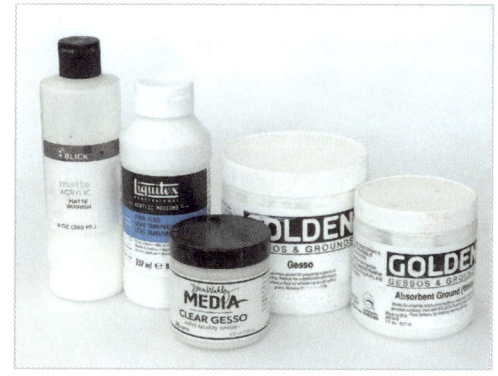

Collage: Much of the collage material I use I make myself. I also use scrapbooking papers, book text, sheet music, tissue paper, mulberry paper, and ledger paper. I like to have a variety of colorful, neutral, and high-contrast collage materials to work with. Light material is key for layering, so you don't want these papers to be too thick. Embellished tissue paper, decorative napkins, and even some wrapping papers are also wonderful for collage.

Ephemera: I like to make my own ephemera too. These are cutout items used to embellish a piece or add a focal point or fun finishing touch to projects. Die cuts and stickers are available in a wide variety from scrapbooking suppliers. Some scrapbooking papers have such lovely imagery that I will fussy-cut to use for ephemera. Washi tape is another standby for embellishing; I love to use ones with metallic detailing for a shimmery touch.

Tools: Pictured here is every tool featured in this book. You'll see various sponges and applicators for applying paint through stencils. I use the hotel key as a scraper or burnishing tool for collage. A pipette comes in handy when my ink droppers get clogged! A skewer is fun to use for adding texture. I love to use a brayer to apply paint, and isn't this one cute? I use a palette knife to spread paint in random ways onto my work. I don't have a favorite brand of brushes, but I always have some inexpensive ones available to use with adhesives. You don't want to use your nice brushes for that. Watercolor brushes are a must for watercolors, and I avoid using these for acrylics to keep them working nicely with the watercolors they are meant for.

Stencils: All the stencils used in this book are from StencilGirl Products. I love these stencils! Stencils add another dimension and take some of the guesswork out of creating for me. When in doubt, use a stencil, I always say!

Mark-makers: For scribbling and adding dark marks and grunge, I use a graphite pencil, a graphite stick, or even oil pastel. (If I use oil pastel, I usually seal all the marks with matte varnish.) To add white marks to darker areas, I use Stabilo All in white, a white oil pastel, or a Caran D'Ache Neocolor I. For outlining and tiny marks, I use a Sakura Gelly Roll pen in white. Sakura Micron pens in black, in various nib sizes, are the main black drawing pen I recommend. I use these for writing and journaling into my mixed-media work, but they're great for doodling and outlining as a finishing touch. To add a little color at the end, I will often add marks using colored pencils, pastels, or paint pens. I like to outline stenciled marks with paint markers too.

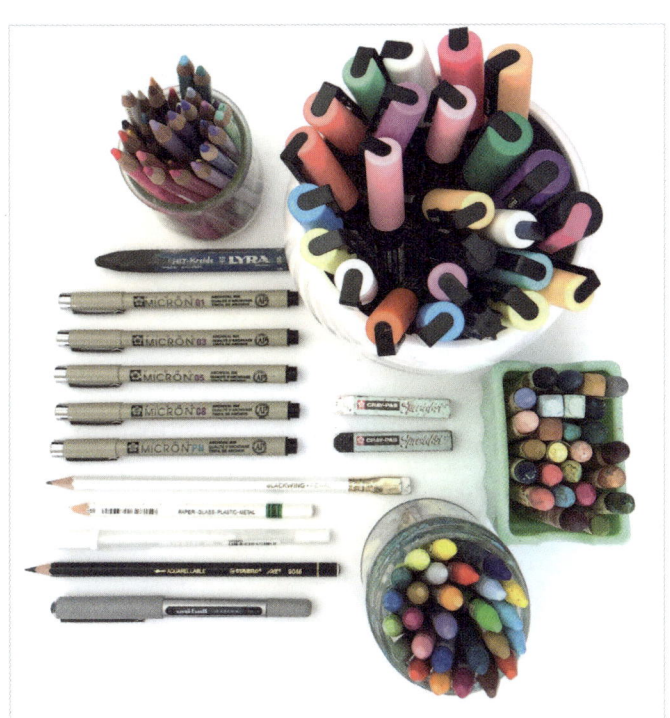

Water-soluble media: It goes without saying that watercolors belong in this family of art supplies. I have pan watercolors, paints in tubes that I dispense into my own tin, and a few fluid watercolors. The ink and dye sprays I use reactivate with water even after they are dry, but they become a little more permanent with time. Finally, in the jars are all my water-soluble mark-makers. They are wonderful for watery applications, but I also use them for mark-making because they are so vibrant. The thick pencils pictured are also highly pigmented. Watercolor pencils from various manufacturers are pictured here.

Inks: India ink (or other fountain pen ink) in black works well for mark-making that you want to stay put. Colored calligraphy ink is a nice option for adding sheer-looking color (similar to watercolor) without worrying if it will be reactivated by wet media in the next layers. I love acrylic inks which are usually opaque instead of sheer because they do not bleed or run when glue is applied over them while collaging. Drops of fluorescent ink add pops of color to projects in the final stages, and I use the metallic or iridescent inks this way too. I often dilute acrylic inks to create a wash to color and unify a layered art paper.

The Art Paper Obsession

One thing was a constant at every Girls' ARTisan Camp I ran: making what I call "art papers," or your own personally created collage paper. The girls at camp would splatter, spray and sponge-paint through stencils, scrape paint onto paper, smoosh their hands in paint and put their handprints on paper, fling around watercolor, and of course, add glitter to these papers. Then we'd create projects out of them. The projects would all have each artist's individual touch because she made the papers that were used to create it.

The trick is not to fall in love with your art papers!

These papers are fun and easy for anyone to make, and none of them are meant to be finished works of art. It's an experiment every time with different variables and outcomes. It is a playful process that can be quite addicting. Letting randomness take over helps you let go of perfectionism.

The trick is not to fall in love with your art papers! I confess I have fallen in love with a few! But that's because they are one-of-a-kind. I've never been able to replicate a layered art paper exactly, even if I follow the same process. But I trust, every time I sit down (or stand up!) to make art papers, I will enjoy the process, and whatever happens, it will be beautiful.

Making these papers is a staple in my creative practice today. I love to layer different media and colors to create vibrant, interesting papers that will inspire me and get me excited to create.

These papers are meant to be torn up and used in other projects. Let them go! Cut them up! Create something new with them! The "something new" that I often create is shareable art because, as you will soon come to know if you do not already, I'm an avid art sharer! Download a few of the art papers created in this book here: juicy-s. net/syj-art-papers. You can print them for your personal use!

MAKING ART PAPERS

Art Paper #1:
Single Color with Texture

To create a pleasing collage composition, I like to have some solid-colored papers to mix in with the printed papers. Art papers featuring a prominent or solid single color with a bit of texture are perfect for this!

Gather Your Supplies

Substrates: newsprint, marker paper, or colored lightweight card stock (such as scrapbooking paper)

Paints: heavy-body acrylics in a few colors from your chosen color palette

Other items: a broad brush (I've used a No. 14), a bamboo skewer, paper towels for drying the brush and cleaning the skewer

TIP

It's a good idea to use papers of varying thickness. In general, because these papers are used in collage, you want fairly thin papers. The colored card stock I've used here is not heavy; everything else is pretty lightweight.

STEP 1

Cover most of a substrate with a thick coat of paint, working quickly so that the paint does not dry. You don't have to cover the paper all the way to the edge.

STEP 2

Use the skewer to scribble overlapping loops into the wet paint. If necessary, clean the skewer periodically on a paper towel so that the paint does not form clumps on the paper.

These papers will take a while to dry. It's best to leave them to dry overnight before using them in a project.

STEP 3

Vary your marks and colors. Make circles instead of scribbling, or make dashes, tick marks, or other marks that you like. Use colored paper, or paint the paper a solid color and let it dry before adding a thick coat of texture to get a bicolored effect.

Art Paper #2:

Patterns of Painty "Marks"

It's amazing what a simple painted mark, repeated in a pattern, can add to a collage composition! Here, you get to make your mark, creating patterned papers with acrylic paintbrush marks. You'll use a few different brush shapes and sizes to get a variety of these "marks." Then use stencils to add shapes. Both colorful, patterned papers will add interest and contrast to your shareable art projects.

Gather Your Supplies

Substrates: suggestions include brown packing paper, newsprint, sulfite paper, book pages, sheet music, a security envelope, and scrapbooking paper (printed and solid color)

Paints: acrylics in a few colors from your chosen color palette

Other items: a paint palette or small dishes to hold paint, a variety of brushes in different shapes and sizes, stencils with small and interesting "marks," and a sponge to apply paint through the stencils

TIP

To clean sponges and stencils, just put them in a sink of warm water and rinse them off. Dry them with a towel or let them air dry. I sometimes let the paint dry on my stencils. But I do reuse my sponges, so I like to get them as clean as possible before paint dries on them.

STEP 1

Choose one color of paint and use a square brush to make brush marks on one of your substrates.

You can cover the whole paper this way, or switch colors along the way.

STEP 2

With a different color of paint and a different substrate, use a small round brush to repeat step 1.

STEP 3

Continue adding brush marks to one or two other substrates. I recommend using black paint on brown packing paper for a dramatic and different look.

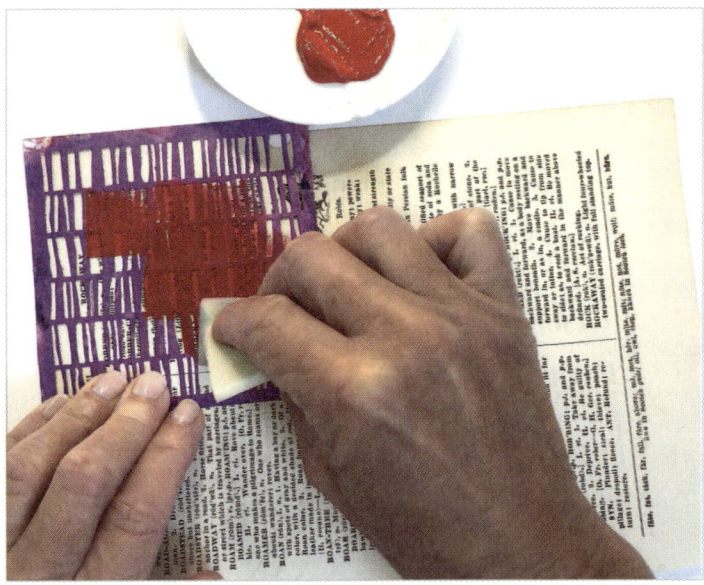

STEP 4

Choose a few stencils to use to add the "marks." Lightly load a sponge with a color of paint, pouncing off any excess onto your paint dish or palette. Apply the sponge gently and straight down onto the stencil to get clean "marks."

STEP 5

Repeat step 4 as many times as you like to create simple but beautiful art papers covered in painty marks.

Art Paper #3:

High-Contrast Doodles

Black is a key ingredient to any art recipe. Just like you want to balance and contrast your food recipes for that perfect flavor profile, adding black can make everything else in your composition pop. These black ink doodles offer contrast as well as interest, and they will help you balance your compositions. Hand-doodled designs make these art papers uniquely you and give your shareable art projects that perfect balance of "flavors."

Gather Your Supplies

Substrates: sketch paper, wide-rule notebook paper, or graph paper

Pens: permanent ink drawing pens in black featuring varying nib widths

NOTE: In this project, I've used Pigma Micron® pens.

TIP

You can test whether the ink in your pen is permanent (not activated by water) by making some test marks on a scrap piece of paper. Go over these marks with a wet paintbrush to see if the ink bleeds. If it doesn't, you know your ink is permanent.

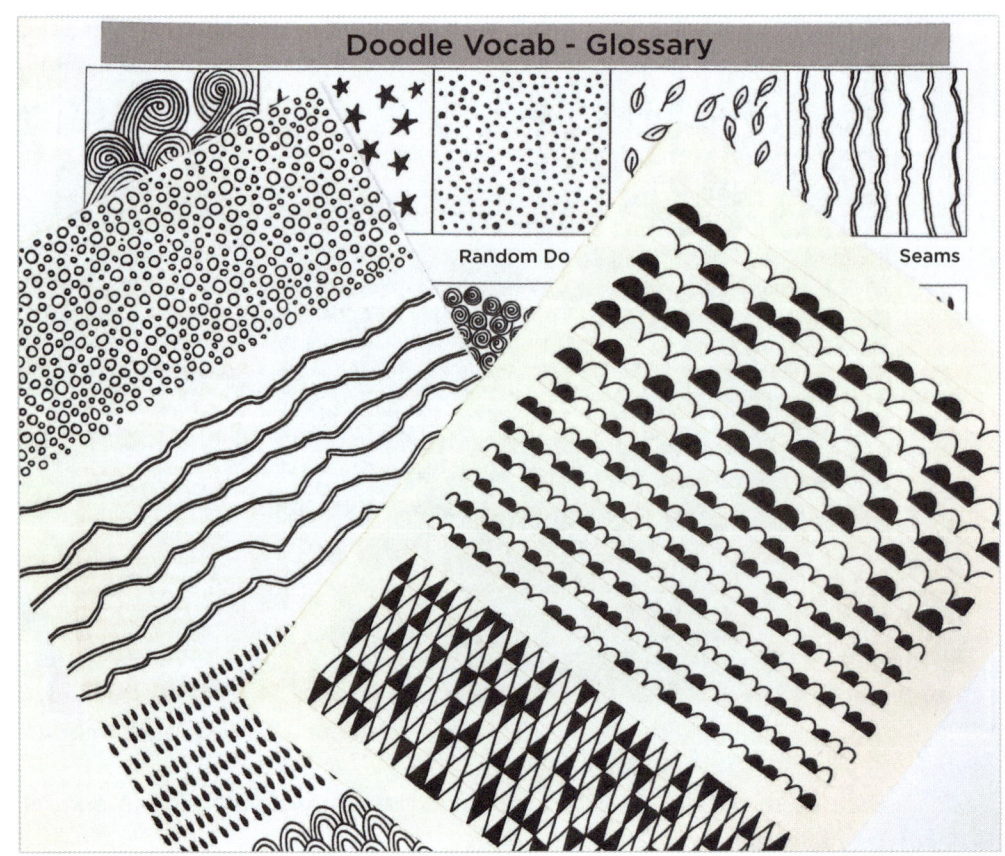

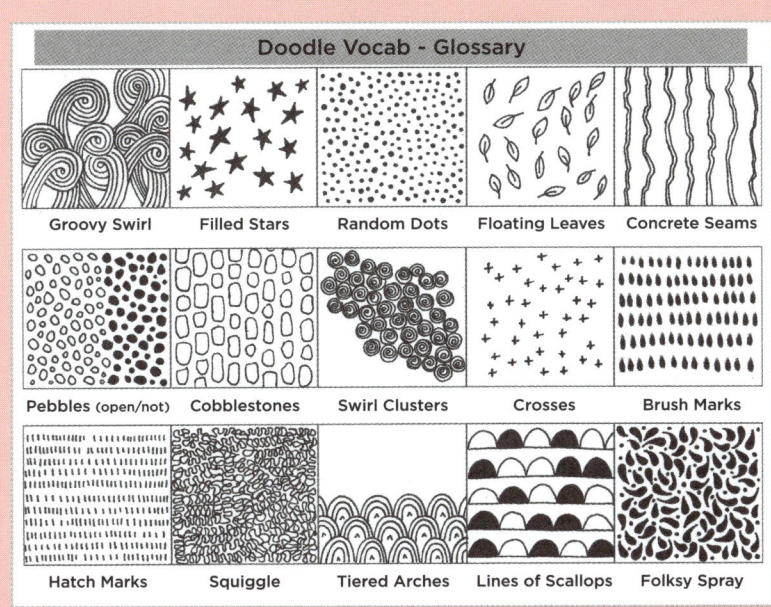

Doodle Vocabulary: Make a Glossary of Your Own Marks

On page 121, you'll find a gridded sheet that you can fill in with ideas for marks. You can then refer to this sheet whenever you need to create art papers like this or add marks to your projects. Here's a photo of a sheet that I've filled in with some of my favorite doodles.

STEP 1

Use your substrate to create doodles, using the lines as guides. As you can see, you don't need to cover the whole page with a single doodle. I like to create sections. If I really love a particular doodle, I'll make that section bigger. I've made scallops in two sizes and a woven pattern using upside-down and right-side up *V*s. Filling in some of the shapes creates higher contrast.

STEP 2

On a piece of paper, create sections of doodles in simple organic shapes.

The possibilities are endless, and the process is quite meditative. This is something I like to do when I'm on the phone or on a video-conference call (that doesn't command my rapt attention!). I just love the high-contrast interest these doodled art papers add to my collage projects!

Art Paper #4:

Tiny Watercolor Marks

The tiny brush marks you can make with watercolors are dainty and beautiful. Art papers created using this technique add an elegant detail to collages and mixed-media projects. Covering an entire sheet of paper with these marks can take a while, so I recommend cutting a sheet of paper in half. This is a very meditative process that I hope you will enjoy.

Gather Your Supplies

Substrates: sulfite paper, marker paper (see Tip)

Watercolors: use a few of your favorite colors that fit with your chosen color palette

Other: jar of water, round #0 watercolor brush, watercolor palette or welled pan case

TIP

Watercolor paper is too heavy for collage; you need substrates that are lightweight but can handle watery media. Marker paper is an option because it is made to receive alcohol markers that may bleed on other paper. Sulfite paper is a light construction paper, but it is sturdy enough for these tiny marks.

STEP 1

Wet your brush, and choose a paint color to load onto your brush. Put the color into a well in your watercolor palette, and then add some water to create a small puddle of color.

STEP 2

Working in sections of different colors, apply tiny brush marks to your substrate in lines across the paper. Start by touching the loaded brush to the paper, and then pull down slightly to make a brush mark. It's okay if your marks are uneven—this just adds interest and shows your hand in creating them!

Art Paper #5:

Sheer Watery Layers

Using water-soluble media (watercolors, crayons, sprays, and inks) to create sheer layers over book text is a fun and easy way to make colorful and interesting art papers for collage. Creating these art papers is an exercise in accepting randomness—watery media, by nature, flow in ways you can't predict. Experiment, play, and see what happens!

Gather Your Supplies

Substrates: book text

Media: water-soluble crayons, shimmer spray (optional), spray inks and dyes or liquid watercolor

Other: dropper or pipette, spray bottle with water, paper towels or rag for blotting

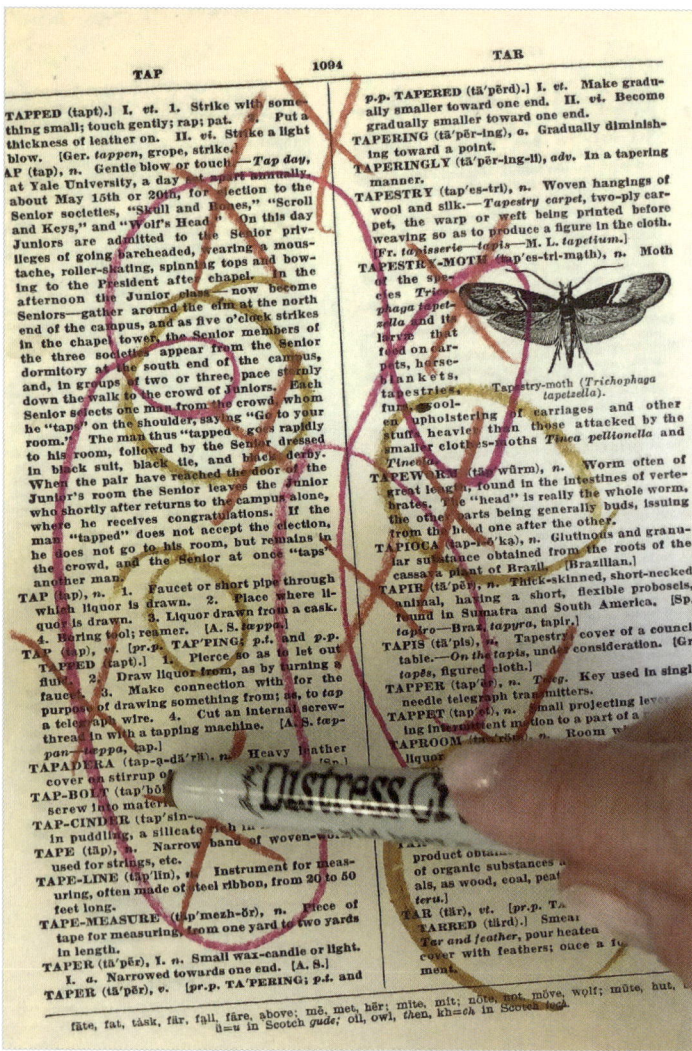

STEP 1

Onto a sheet of book text, make some scribbly marks with water-soluble crayons in two or three colors.

STEP 2

Spritz some shimmer spray onto the book page. This will start to activate the water-soluble crayons. If you don't have shimmer spray, skip this step.

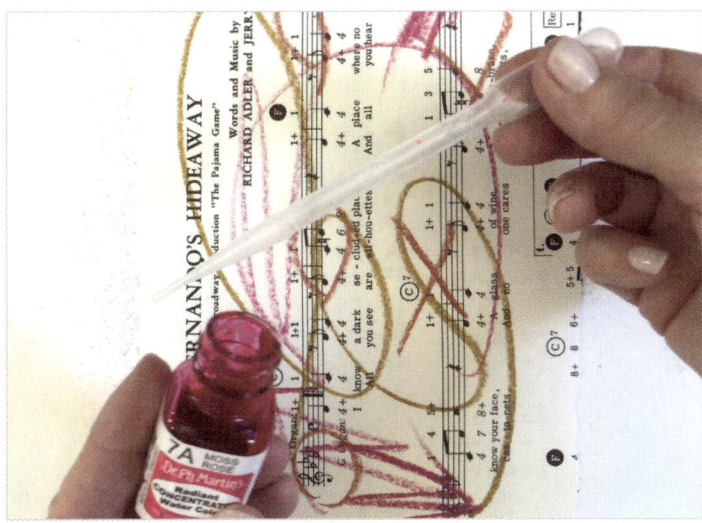

STEP 3

Spray the substrate with one or two different colors of ink or dye spray in a couple spots. At this point, there should still be some white space showing on your substrate. If you don't have ink or dye sprays, you can make your own by filling a small spray bottle about halfway with water and adding five to six full droppers of concentrated watercolor to the bottle.

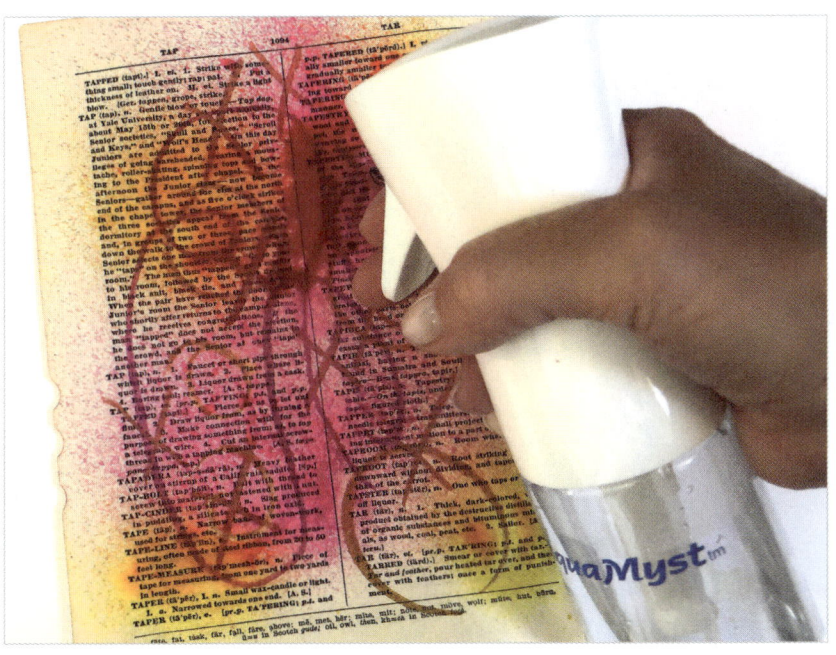

STEP 4

Spray the entire substrate with water to activate the crayons and make the watercolor and sprays flow. The paper should not be totally soaked; wet it just enough to get things running together a little.

STEP 5

Repeat steps 1 through 4 on different book pages. Try some different color combinations. When you get to step 4, you can move the paper to get the flow going into areas that may not yet have color, or just leave a little white space on your paper. If too much water pools in some areas, blot the water with a paper towel. Let this art paper dry thoroughly before using in any of your projects.

TAP (tap), n. Gentle blow or touch. —T at Yale University, a day set apart as about May 15th or 20th, for election of Senior societies, "small and famed," Juniors are admitted to the Senior-leges of going bareheaded, wearing tache, roller-skating, spinning tops and ing to the President on the... afternoon the pair have reached the door Seniors—rather around the elm at the end of the campus, and an eye of clock down the walk to the crowd of... Senior selects one man from the crowd he "tap on the shoulder, saying... man "tapped" does not accept the... he goes not go to his room, the Senior men to another man.

TAP (tap), n. 1. Faucet or short pipe which liquor is drawn. 2. Place gut is drawn. 3. Liquor. [A. S. *tæppe...* 2. Boring tool; reamer. [A. S. *tæppe.*]

TAPPED (tapt), *pp.* [*pr.* **TAP'PING**; *p.t.,* find. 2. Draw liquor from, as by tap fauces...

THE BRYOPH...

tissue stretched across from the t... skin a drum (the epiphragma) the pores between adjacent te... vegetative reproduction by ge... clusters of cells or multic... stalked gemmae of *Tetr... is (g...* and stems can also regenerate...

Classification

The main subdivisions of the B... early investigations or minor cha... of the groups have and will contin... series of sub-classes seems to be a...

Sphagnidae (*Sphagnum*)
  Sphagnales
  Andreaeidae (*Andreæa...*
    Andreaeales
  Bryidae. The subdivis...

Chi-S

$P(0) = ...45...$
$P(1) = 4(...$
$P(2) = 6(55...$
$P(3) = 4(5...$
$P(4) = (.55...$

The binomial distribution with

Multiplying each of these pr...
expected numbers of occurren...
$40.1, 3675(200) = 73.5, 2995.$

Expected number of days

0
8.2

FACTOR (fak'tUr), *a.* 1. One who buys and sell goods for others. 2. One of two or more quantities, which, multiplied together, form a product. 3. One of the circumstances or causes that produce a result [L. from *factum,* *fac,* of *facio,* make.]

FACTOR (fak'tUr), *v.* [*pr.p.* **FAC'TORING**; *p... and *pp.* **FACTORED** (fak'tUrd...*]* 1. *t.* ... as factors. 2. *Math.* Resolve into factors, into factors.

FACTORIAL (fak-to'ri-al), *a.* Of or pertaining to a factor or a factory.

FACTORY (fak'tUr-i), *n.* [*pl.* **FAC'TORIES.**] Manufactory; building for manufacturing. 2. Business place of a factor, especially in eastern countries.

FACTOTUM (fak-to'tum), *n.* Person employed to do all kinds of work. [L., do all.]

FACULE (fak'ūl), *n.pl. Astron.* Certain spots sometimes seen on the sun's disk, which appear brighter than the rest of its surface. [L. *facula,* dim. of *fax,* torch.]

FACULTATIVE (fak'ul-tā-tiv), *a.* 1. Bestow... ing right or power. 2. *Bot.* Optional o... incidental.

FACULTY (fak'ul-ti), *n. [pl.* **FAC'ULTIES.**] 1. Power of the mind; personal quality or endowment. 3. Privilege; license. 4. Body of teachers. [L. *facultas...*] fession. 5. Body of teachers. [L. *facultas,* *facilis,* easy.]

FAD (fad), *n.* Weak hobby; popular whim... [Fr. *fade,* insipid.]

FADDIST (fad'ist), *n.* One who is a slave... some fad.

FADDLE (fad'l), *n.* Nonsense; usually...

A7   D

were   small?

---

lieu d'être su... Danube. Jaloux
hiduc Charles... nouré d'un état-
état-major général... l'avait... vé
ation sur le plan à suivre... v...
r directement dans le Tyrol... le
passant les sources de la Drave
Adige (voir la carte nº 31), descen-
Trente sur Vérone, et faire tom-
s défenses avancées des Français,
trait sur la ligne de l'Adige par la
nes, que lui ouvrait l'insurrection
ayant pas la crainte de trouver
Rivoli le général Bonaparte ou
a, pouvant compter sur le con-

RATISBONNE

archiduc Charles réuni à... arm...
se... la... de Hiller et d...
l'avantage... ouvrir...
défendaient tou... us 36...
moralisés, d'avoir... ris l'hu...
filés de la Bohême, où ce c...
sé pour long-temps, d'avoir...
s environ 60 mille hom...
ces de canon Sur ces 60...
ait été atteints p...
e sabre de nos ca...

MAKING ART PAPERS

Art Paper #6:

Wistful Watercolor

Watercolors can be full of saturated color or sheer and light in color depending on how much water you add to them. The more water you add, the less control you have, so the pigment flows in unpredictable ways. The art papers we create here can be used as backgrounds for postcards and artist trading cards because you are working on watercolor paper, a heavier and sturdier substrate.

Gather Your Supplies

Substrates: watercolor paper (at least 300 g or 130 lb)

Media: watercolors (pan, tube, or liquid)

Other: spray bottle with water, #10 watercolor brush, jar of water, watercolor paint palette or small dishes, coarse salt, wax paper

Watercolor Clouds

STEP 1

Using a spray bottle filled with water, spray one piece of watercolor paper to wet it thoroughly before applying paint.

STEP 2

Wet your paintbrush and dip it into a color, and then apply the paint to the paper in "clouds," adding water or more paint to your brush to get the paint to flow. Cover a few areas on the paper with one color. Apply a different color in the same way. It's okay if the colors run together a little at the edges. Repeat this process once more with a third color. Add water—not more paint— to your brush to get lighter variations of the same color. Keep adding "clouds" in the three different colors until the paper is completely covered. (Alternatively, you can leave small amounts of white space between some of the clouds.)

STEP 3

If your paper starts to dry out during your painting session, spray the dry areas with water, or just load your brush with water from your jar and brush it onto the dry spots.

Salty Watercolor

STEP 1

Wet your watercolor paper thoroughly before adding paint. Dip it into a cool color, and then apply the paint in a stripe across the paper. Add water and/or paint to your brush to get the paint to flow, creating a stripe with a width of about 2 inches (5 cm) in one color.

STEP 2

Repeat step 1 to apply a different cool color next to the first stripe of color. It's okay if the colors run together a little. Continue the process of adding cool colors, or repeat one or two colors, until the paper is covered. Work fairly quickly so the paint doesn't have time to dry. If the surface appears dry, lightly mist it with water. From a small bowl or the palm of your hand, pinch some salt between your fingers and sprinkle it over the wet paper. You'll immediately see how the watercolor flows away from the salt crystals. Let this dry completely.

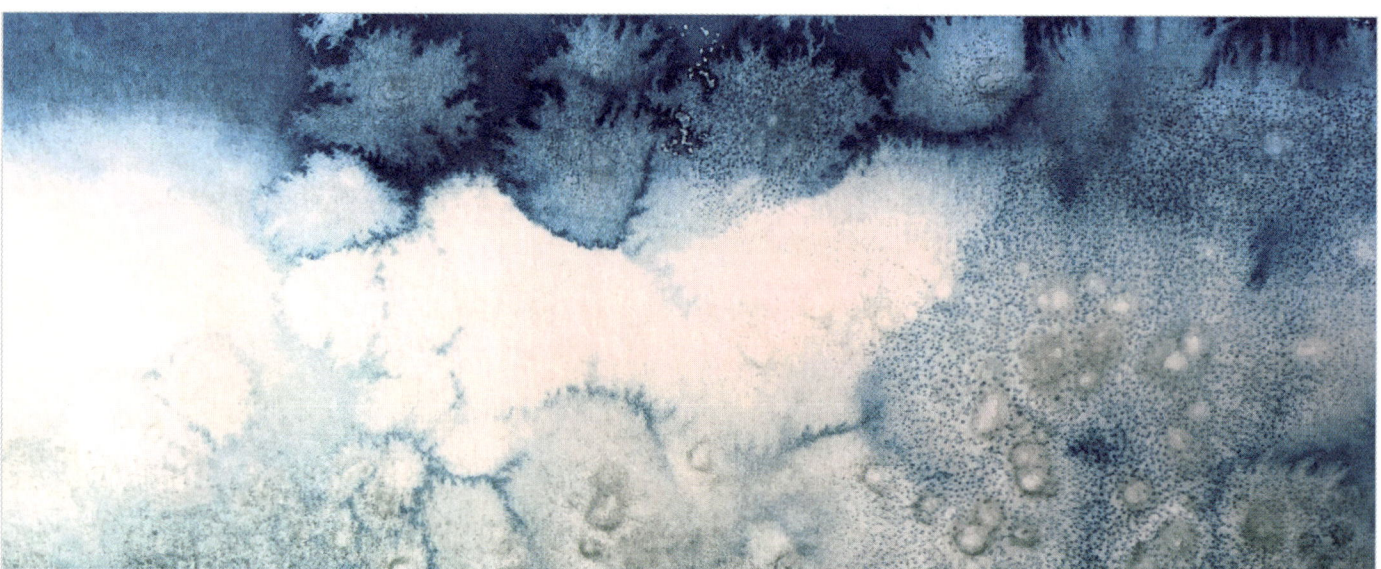

STEP 3

When the paper is dry, rub off the salt, revealing a pattern of starry spots where the salt grabbed the water and color from the paper.

Wax Paper Texture

STEP 1

Apply watercolor to another piece of paper using steps 1 through 3 in Salty Watercolor (page 34). Try warm colors or mix it up. A rainbow always looks nice! If the paint seems to have dried once the paper is covered with color, spray a thin mist of water over the entire surface.

STEP 2

While the paper is still wet, crumple up a piece of wax paper and smoosh it down onto the paint. If one piece of crumpled wax paper won't cover the entire watercolor surface, crumple up a few more to cover it. Weigh down the crumpled wax paper with a few handy objects so that it stays in contact with the watercolor surface. Leave the whole thing to dry thoroughly.

STEP 3

When the paper is dry, remove the wax paper to reveal an uneven textured effect.

Art Paper #7:

Playing with Inks

Inks are a standby for me because they have great pigment, are very fluid, and dry permanently. I use them in all sorts of ways, but one that I love is, of course, random and playful. When you're dripping ink or drawing with the end of a dropper, you can't predict or plan, so you have no choice but to let go of perfection! I also like to use drawing inks and acrylic inks as paint with a watercolor brush to create loose marks and imagery to cut out and use as focal points in collage projects.

Gather Your Supplies

Substrates: newsprint, sulfite construction paper, book text, ledger, or lined paper

Paints: acrylic inks (with droppers) in a few colors from your chosen color palette, including an iridescent or metallic ink—include black or another dark like Paynes gray; high-flow acrylic paints; drawing or writing inks, such as India ink, or fountain pen ink

STEP 1

Choose a substrate and a color of acrylic ink. Use the tip of the dropper to make marks onto the paper. Apply a slight amount of pressure to the dropper bulb to release ink gradually as you move the end of the dropper over the paper. You want the ink to flow as you move the dropper end, but you don't want a flood of ink making a puddle on your paper. Start with circles as a good warm-up. This green iridescent ink is not only colorful, but it also has a shimmer that adds even more dimension.

STEP 2

You can make any marks you like. Use your imagination and let the inks flow without thinking too much about how the art paper will turn out. It's okay if shapes bump up against each other and the ink flows together. Taking your time and going slowly gives you a little more control for shapely patterns.

STEP 3

Once you are warmed up, try moving more loosely and quickly to create shapes with some flair and movement.

STEP 4

Painting with inks is another way to play with them. Using a watercolor brush and acrylic ink, high-flow acrylic, or drawing ink, we can create inky marks or even ephemera (focal point imagery). Dispense some ink into a small dish or in one well of your watercolor paint palette. If you're using acrylic ink or high-flow acrylic paint, wet your brush and add a little water to the ink/acrylic to give it a more watery consistency. If you are using India ink or fountain pen ink, do not dilute these. With your brush loaded with ink, create bold marks and strokes across the paper.

STEP 5

You can create bold circles, connected painty marks, or even scribble with the brush to create unreadable writing.

STEP 6

Use a dark ink to create shapes that you can cut out and use as ephemera in your projects. These simple bold leaves are going to add interest and contrast to an abstract collage. Let all your papers dry thoroughly before using them.

MAKING ART PAPERS

Art Paper #8:

Stenciled Layers

One of my mixed media mottos is, "When in doubt, use a stencil!" I often play with stencils by creating layered art papers to use in collage or layered backgrounds in my art journal. One technique that is consistent for each of these layered papers is to use only parts of the stencil to add marks in random spots over the substrate. Using ink in a color I love to add a wash over the layers of stenciled marks can finish and transform these papers in a magical way!

Gather Your Supplies

Substrates: sulfite paper, book text, vintage ledger, neutral scrapbooking paper, security envelope, or sheet music

Paints: acrylic paints from your chosen color palette, acrylic ink in a color you love

Other: paint palette, stencils, sponge for stenciling, paintbrush (I used a ¾-inch [2 cm] wash)

STEP 1

Dispense several colors of acrylic paint onto your paint palette. Select a substrate and a stencil. For the first stencil layer, work with one of your darker colors. Use a sponge or other applicator to pick up some paint; blot it a little so you don't have excess paint on the sponge, then pounce through the stencil in random areas on the substrate. Repeat this process, adding stenciling onto random areas all over the substrate. If you have a lot of paint left on your sponge, off-load it onto your substrate by adding a few areas of solid color adjacent to the stencil marks.

STEP 2

Repeat step 1 several more times using a different stencil and a different paint color with each stencil layer. Randomly stencil over your substrate, overlapping existing stencil marks.

STEP 3

To add the acrylic ink wash, dispense a small amount of acrylic ink color into a watercolor palette well or a small dish. Wet the brush and transfer water to the ink, adding about the same amount of water as ink to the dish. You might need several brushloads of water to achieve the proper consistency. Then, brush the ink over the entire surface of your stenciled paper.

Shareable Art:
The Power of Paying Art Forward

I've always been a pay-it-forward kind of person, and that's why I love shareable art. Sharing my art keeps me inspired to create, and it's helped me learn how to make mixed-media work. Over the past thirteen years, I've swapped postcards, traded artist trading cards, exchanged paper scraps, swapped art journals, and gifted my art to strangers, friends, and family.

The truth is, I've given a lot of my art away. This is partly a way of practicing letting go, not grasping and holding onto things. Setting them free, saying goodbye, and being okay with not having them in a collection—these are all ways to practice mindful detachment.

Besides, the making of it is what gives me joy! Once a thing is made, where does it go? Stored in my art closet? I would rather have it out in the world spreading joy to someone else while I make more! I love creating—the process of using my hands and imagination to transform art supplies into something beautiful. The end product gets a whole new life when I share it with someone else. Giving something so full of creative energy and love is, to me, sharing my joy. It's also a way of creating real connections.

The Shareable Projects

Each of the projects featured here is something I have made and sent away. They'll all fit into an envelope and make it to their destinations through the postal service. It's a simple, beautiful, analog way of sharing and connecting that is actually quite powerful. I think you can envision the delighted faces of the recipients when they go to their mailboxes and see one of these envelopes!

I hope you enjoy the process of making these shareable projects. My wish is that you will find joy in creating and sending them and that whoever receives your creations feels all that joy!

Postcards

For many years, the only art I set aside time to do was making postcards. When you're working and in mom-mode, it's not always easy to find time to bust out the art supplies and take some creative time for yourself.

Small art like postcards seemed more manageable, and it was. As added motivation, I was participating in iHanna's DIY Postcard Swap. I had agreed to make and send cards to ten different people, and they were counting on receiving my cards! The postcards I've received over the years are beautiful, playful, hilarious, ingenious, fun, and totally one-of-a-kind.

Years of committing to sending postcards helped me develop as an artist. I got to experiment, play, and try new things. I started a blog and posted about how I created my cards, wanting to share my process. The process, I discovered, is the most meaningful thing about creating, and in that process, I was experiencing joy! Sharing my creations took that joy to another level.

One of the most wonderful things about swapping postcards is the connections I've made. In this digital age of sharing online via social media, the postcard remains my tried-and-true snail-mail connection to many of the artists in my mixed-media community. The swap happens twice a year, and you can read more about Hanna and the postcard exchange on page 59.

Because the possibilities are basically endless in mixed media, there are many ways to create mixed media art postcards. One easy and fun way is to make a larger work that is then cut into postcard-size pieces. I think it's actually kind of magical what can happen when you cut that larger piece: beautiful, unintentional compositions; little hints of a particular color; a splatter in the corner that catches your eye; the mystery and wonder of what could be on another card. It really gives me joy!

Shareable Project #1:
Sewn Collage Postcards

We made these cards almost every single summer at Girls' ARTisan Camp. Each camper would collage their art papers, scrapbooking papers, magazine cutouts (lots of animals!), and embellishing ephemera onto a blank sheet of paper. Then I would run the collages through my sewing machine using different colors of thread to give the collages detail and texture. Finally, I'd cut up the collages, sew the cut pieces onto postcard backs or folded note card fronts, and bundle them up with envelopes and a ribbon. Each camper received her sewn bundle at the end of camp and could use the cards as special greetings and thank-you notes throughout the year. These are beautiful, one-of a-kind, shareable art cards that everyone is delighted to receive!

Gather Your Supplies

Substrate: 11" × 14" (28 × 36 cm) paper, such as lightweight mixed-media paper or heavier drawing paper

Collage materials: art papers, scrapbooking papers, origami papers, magazine cutouts, printed wrapping paper, washi tape, embellishing ephemera

Other: glue stick, sewing machine, various colors of sewing machine thread (optional), paper trimmer (or scissors, pencil, and ruler)

Finishing: card stock for postcard backing, envelopes for mailing, postcard back label from the pullout on page 123

STEP 1

Part of the work for this project is choosing the collage materials you're going to use. If you've created all the art papers in this book, you will have quite a selection! If you haven't yet made the art papers, I recommend making AP1, AP2, AP3, AP4, and AP5. You'll want to use papers that are lightweight, not card-stock weight. Gather a range of tones—lighter, medium, and darker—plus papers with less detail, some with solid colors, and others that have more detail. Here, I chose some scrapbooking papers and art papers that went well with them. I chose some book text and some vintage sheet music that add a neutral tone and provide spaces to add imagery like magazine cutouts or ephemera in the second collage layer.

STEP 2

First collage layer: Using a glue stick, adhere small pieces of your selected collage materials in a grid over the entire surface of the substrate. I like to tear up some papers into small squares and rectangles before I start to collage, and then I adjust the size by tearing them down further as I work. You can overlap pieces slightly. Feel free to throw in a larger piece or much smaller piece here and there to fill in blank spots and make it look a little less uniform.

STEP 3

Washi tape layer: To help define the postcards, I roughly measured where the cards will be cut and placed the washi tape in a strip along what will be the cards' edges. I added tape in other areas, overlapping the edges of some of the collage pieces to unify the collage. I like to add metallic tape and other colors that will complement my collage.

STEP 4

Focal points layer: Look through your magazine cutouts and choose some to adhere as "focal points" throughout the collage. For the most part, I like to fussy-cut (see Tip) my magazine imagery. For words or phrases, I trim them down as close to the letters as possible so that more of my collage will show.

I suggest using eight main focal images (the collage will be cut into eight 3.5" × 5" [9 × 13-cm] postcards). You don't want to cover up too much of the collage, and you want these additional collage elements to pop. If there's too much going on, they may get lost. I like to adhere the focal point layer of collage in a fairly random way, but I do have a general idea of how the cards will be oriented once I cut them out. Apart from any words or phrases, I'm not too concerned about making sure the whole cutout will show up on a postcard—I like to see what surprises show up as I'm cutting the collage into cards! Sometimes a focal image might be on the cut line and show up on two separate postcards. If you're concerned, you could use a piece of 3.5" × 5" (9 × 13 cm) paper to cover the collage and see where your images are falling. I recommend doing this for words and phrases.

Fussy-cutting is cutting closely around all the contours of an image, such as the petals of a flower; this can take practice. Here are my tricks: First, using a larger pair of scissors seems counterintuitive, but it's efficient because the blades are longer and you don't have to actually "scissor" as much. Second, turn the piece of magazine or paper to move around the outline instead of working the scissors around. Lastly, look where you want to go instead of where your scissors are cutting; keep your eyes slightly ahead of the cut you're making and it will be easier.

STEP 5

Once you have your focal points down, you have the option of adding some embellishing ephemera. These can be flat stickers, die-cuts, or words and phrases. (Check Resources on page 118 for some sources for these items.) You can see some gold-foil hearts, acetate butterflies, and paper die-cuts in my collage. I usually adhere these items next to the focal points already in the collage so they're anchored by the focal point and not floating in space; once the cards are cut up, pleasing compositions will appear! Try to avoid embossed, resin, or puffy items—they will be in the way if you sew your collage and may not mail that well.

STEP 6

Now it's time to sew! Before sewing, make sure that all the glue in your collage has thoroughly dried. I like to use three or four different thread colors and use a straight stitch and a zigzag stitch. For the most part, you want to keep the stitches on a longer stitch setting; I recommend a stitch length setting of 4. Too small and you risk perforating the paper too much, and it may tear. Also, a wider stitch just shows up a bit better. Sometimes I'll sew outlines or frames around focal points or words in the collage to accentuate them. This step is all about adding dimension, interest, and a little more color to your collage. If you don't have a sewing machine, just skip this step.

STEP 7

Trim any excess thread from your collage. Using a paper trimmer (or measure with a pencil and ruler, and use scissors), cut the collage into postcards. Along the long edge, cut the collage into 3.5-inch (9 cm) pieces. Then cut each of these four pieces into two 5-inch (13 cm) pieces. Hold on to any scraps! Nothing goes to waste in mixed media. (I had some pretty little scraps that I knew I could use for some woven ATCs.)

Finally, cut eight pieces of plain card stock a little larger than your postcards. To sew the collage pieces to the card stock pieces, make a straight stitch around the edges using a thread color that coordinates with your collage. You can glue the two pieces together first, but tack them at the center with a small amount of glue so you don't end up sewing through glue. I like to leave a border of about ⅛ inch (3 mm) between the stitching and the edges of the cards. If your card stock isn't exactly the same size as the collage piece, trim the card stock edges.

STEP 8

Write your greeting on the back and leave room for a stamp and the recipient's address, or use the whole blank back to write and then send the card in an envelope. I usually use an envelope. If I have time, I embellish the envelopes so my recipients know there's art mail inside! (I show you how to make some embellished envelopes on page 112.)

If you are not sewing, adhere the card stock backing with a glue stick, making sure to get glue all the way to the edges of the card. If your card stock pieces are slightly larger than the collage pieces, you can trim them once the glue has dried.

Postcard Backs

Included in one of the pullouts (page 123) is a postcard back you can cut from the page or copy, scan, and print. Print this onto card stock and sew or glue it to your cut postcards. But postcard backs are optional if you feel your cards are sturdy enough. On the blank back of the card, you can write your message, add three lines to the right side for the recipient's address, and add postage!

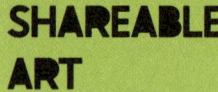

SHAREABLE ART

Shareable Project #2:

Painted Layers Postcards

Let's make some unique mixed-media postcards! First, we conquer the blank page by collaging some high-contrast papers onto our substrate. Then we add some unifying gesso, followed by water-soluble media, paint, inks, and mark-makers. We then cut the big piece into postcards, and unexpected beauty emerges. Let's play!

Gather Your Supplies

Substrate: 11" × 14" (28 × 36 cm) heavyweight paper (such as Bristol or watercolor paper, at least 100 lb/270 gsm)

Collage materials: high-contrast art papers (black and white AP3)

Paints: acrylic paints from your chosen color palette or several that go together nicely

Media: watercolor crayons or pencils, shimmer spray, water-soluble ink spray

Acrylic inks: black to add contrast, metallic ink to add interest, an additional color that coordinates with your color palette to use as a wash (this color will be a dominant color wherever you use it, so make sure you like it!)

Mark-makers: crayons, pencil, Stabilo All (black), paint pens, black-ink drawing pens (Micron 05), gel pens (white Sakura Gelly Roll)

Other: matte medium, several paintbrushes in different sizes, gesso, rag or baby wipe, stencil, dropper, small dish or welled paint palette, water jug, paper trimmer (or pencil, ruler, and scissors), found words or phrases

STEP 1

Randomly place several pieces of high-contrast collage material over your substrate. Apply a thin layer of matte medium to the substrate and then a thin coat over the collaged piece, using the brush to burnish the collage and remove air bubbles. (I use a cheap brush that I don't care about getting glue on.) This layer will get mostly covered up, but some of the dark markings show through other layers later on and give your work depth and interest.

STEP 2

Cover the entire substrate and all the collage pieces with a thin layer of gesso and a bigger brush (I used a broad #14). You'll immediately notice how this layer of see-through paint brings the composition into a unified whole. If the gesso is too thick in some areas and you can't see through it, use a damp rag or baby wipe to blot some of the gesso off the collage.

STEP 3

Use a water-soluble crayon to scribble and mark up the sheet. The color you choose should be one that will inform later color choices and become a theme for your postcards. Concentrate color in some areas, and leave lines and marks in other areas. Spray a few spots with a shimmer spray or other water-soluble ink spray to get the color flowing. Use a medium wet brush (such as a Filbert #12) to activate the water-soluble crayon and spread out some of the spray.

STEP 4

For the first acrylic paint layer, choose a light to medium tone and paint irregular-shaped blobs in random spots over the piece. Use a medium brush for this (such as the Filbert #12). A good rule of thumb is to place the paint blobs in areas between pieces of the collage in the first layer. This "joins" the pieces and covers the blank areas, and you don't have to second-guess where to put this paint.

STEP 5

For the second acrylic paint layer, use your favorite color from your chosen color palette. Use a slightly smaller brush (I used a Filbert #6) to apply this paint in the same way, but make these painted areas slightly bigger than the blobs in step 4. Use a scrubbing technique with your brush to give the edges of these painted areas a feathered, fuzzy look.

STEP 6

For the third acrylic paint layer, choose a lighter-colored paint. Place a small amount of the paint onto a piece of scrap paper. Place this scrap paper paint-side down, using your fingers to press the paper and "smoosh" paint onto your piece in random spots. Because this paint is lighter, use it in areas where there is still white space showing. This provides a pop of brightness and some unpredictable marks.

STEP 7

For the final acrylic paint layer, use a stencil and a darker paint to sponge some shapes in random areas over the piece. Place the stencil going off the edge of the piece, as well as overlapping some of the existing paint layers. It's a darker paint, so it will show up over the other paint colors already there.

STEP 8

Add some black acrylic ink drops by filling the ink bottle dropper with acrylic ink. Apply very slight pressure to the dropper bulb to splatter the ink onto your piece. To avoid giant puddles of ink, I shake the dropper toward the substrate instead of squeezing the ink onto the piece. It's like you're throwing ink at your piece instead of purposely "dropping" it from the dropper. Let the ink drops dry thoroughly before going to step 9.

STEP 9

Use a small round brush (I used a round #1) to make brush marks with the metallic ink. The iridescent jade green I chose stands out on some of the darker layers of paint. Let these marks dry completely before moving on to step 10.

STEP 10

Place a dropper full of colored ink into a small dish or paint palette with wells. Load up a medium brush (I used the Filbert #12) with water and add this to the dish. Repeat three or four times so you have equal amounts of water and ink. Mix the water into the ink and load your brush with diluted ink. Create striations and lines across some of the lighter painted areas to create interest and contrast. Do not cover the entire piece with this wash, and blot it off your piece if it seems to cover too much.

STEP 11

After the wash dries, create doodles and scribbles. First, scribble across the whole piece with a soft graphite pencil. Then, make some marks with a crayon (water soluble or not). I like to think of my crayon bubbles as meandering over the piece.

STEP 12

Using a paper trimmer (or a pencil, ruler, and scissors), cut the collage into postcards. Along the long edge, cut the collage into four 3.5-inch (9 cm) pieces. Then cut each of these pieces into two 5-inch (13 cm) pieces. Now you have eight postcards. Keep any scraps to cut into narrower strips for the Woven Paper Artist Trading Cards on page 68.

STEP 13

To add some fun, cut out found words and phrases from an old book. I have a few books with larger type that I use just for this purpose! Adhere the phrases to your cards. If you feel that your cards could use a little reinforcement, add a postcard back. See step 7 in the Sewn Collage Postcards project on page 50.

Hanna Andersson

Hanna Andersson lives in beautiful Sweden. Known as iHanna online, she is a mixed-media artist, blogger, and writer who has been sharing her creative journey online since 2004. She writes a blog, creates tutorials, and posts videos to share her interests and her creative process.

As an artist, Hanna works mainly in books, but she is also a bookbinder and creates eclectic junk journals and other handmade goods to sell.

When the DIY Postcard Swap had its tenth anniversary, Hanna created a book about its rich history from blog posts and years of photographing her many piles of shared art.

You can find out more about Hanna, read her blog, and sign up for her newsletter to be alerted when the next postcard swap begins. Visit her website at www.ihanna. nu. She also shares her colorful world on Instagram at @ihannas.

The iHanna DIY Postcard Swap by Hanna Andersson

Hi! I'm Hanna, host of the DIY Postcard Swap. There is such immense joy in creative expression. This feeling increases as we share that joy with others. My longing to express myself is one of the many reasons I try to do something creative every day.

Ever since I started playing with mixed-media art, I have also needed outlets to share it. First, I started a blog (which is still going strong), and then I came to YouTube, Instagram, and eventually swaps. I found a lot of one-to-one swap opportunities through the image-sharing site Flickr, where we would post pictures of the artist trading cards we created. Anyone could claim them and ask if they were "available" to trade through the mail. When a friend and art blogger hosted a one-time handmade postcard swap, I was so inspired that I wanted to create more postcards, which eventually led to starting my own postcard swap. I was overwhelmed by how many wanted to join, but every time someone sends me a postcard or an email thanking me for hosting this event, I feel that it is worth the time I put into it.

Swaps gave me the opportunity to not only share what I make but also to get my hands on others' creations, study them closely, and feel more connected to other creators.

To me, my art is a kind of self-portrait. In a swap, we are sharing these small pieces of ourselves with potential new friends from all over the world.

I coined the expression "DIY Postcard" in 2010 when I started iHanna's DIY Postcard Swap. I ran, and still host, the swap from my blog, Studio iHanna.

DIY postcards are handmade, "do-it-yourself" postcards. It's your chance to experiment with themes, colors, art materials, and subject matter in a series and then share it with the world.

It is exciting to dare to share your art, to let it be seen, and to give it away. You can create postcards in any way that inspires you. Being a beginner might even be a benefit if you can cultivate your childlike curiosity and a humble attitude toward what comes out. When I made my first collaged postcards, I had no idea what I was doing, and everyone who got one was still kind and awesome about it—they too had been beginners once.

DIY postcards have been my focus for many years, and to me, they're the ultimate shareable art form. I run my swap twice a year. It is an international swap, and hundreds of people from all continents have joined through the years. Many participants tell me they look forward to the DIY postcard swap every time I host it.

You sign up for the swap and create your cards. Then, I send you the list of your swappers and their addresses. I try to make it so that everyone has as many different countries as possible on their list because even though the cost of international postage is higher, it's always extra exciting to get postcards from other countries.

In my swap, I challenge participants to create ten handmade postcards in any style they wish. When you sign up for a swap, you get a deadline (this helps solve the problem of *when* to start because there will be a delivery deadline). You will have people expecting your art, so if you're a procrastinator or a bit fearful of jumping in, this is the perfect way to get started with shareable art. Plus, you will be sending your efforts to potential new friends, people who are also interested in mixed-media art and are happy to share their own efforts. You find your people.

One of the things I personally love about handmade postcards is the fact that you don't need to pack them before sending them. You simply write the message on the back of the art, add a mailing address and a stamp, and it's ready. It will be exposed to postal handling and stamping, be seen by many postal workers, and may even be exposed to the weather before it arrives at its destination in a new kind of state. I think it is exciting to consider that journey—how the

postcards I create will travel to new countries I have never been to.

Creating and sending out your DIY postcards is the first big step toward a new adventure, but the excitement does not end there. A few days or weeks after sending your mail art, you will start receiving handmade postcards in your own mailbox. You will get painted, collaged, doodled, sewn, and very colorful and exciting mail for days. Some you will love so much you will want to hang them on the fridge or even frame them, and you can because they're yours to keep. This might get you so excited that you will continue to create, share, and be part of the swapping community for years to come. That is what happened to me, and over a decade later, I am still in love with the entire process of making art and sharing it.

Artist Trading Cards

Artist trading cards originated in a conceptual art project started by Swiss artist M. Vänçi Stirnemann in 1997. Dubbed a "collaborative cultural performance," Stirnemann exhibited 1,200 ATCs and offered to trade with anyone who wanted to create an ATC of their own. Stirnemann's collaborative project was intended to equalize the art playing field, allowing people to participate in an ongoing art project with no prerequisite of being an "artist" recognized in the art market.

As such, it referenced earlier art movements such as Dadaism and Mail Art. Dadaism was a movement of artists rejecting the commercialization of art and a tongue-in-cheek protest of the way capitalism placed monetary value on art. This movement sought to bring the ordinary and everyday into art by making art of these things, thereby making "art" an inside joke.

The Mail Art movement of the 1960s took this philosophy a step further as an egalitarian way of creating that could circumvent chains of official art distribution and evaluation. Mail Art was a network of fellow creators exchanging art in the mail, completely removed from the "art market" and independent from the burden of locating and securing exhibition space.

Just like postcards, the mixed-media ATC possibilities are limitless. The substrate is smaller—strictly speaking, an ATC must be 2.5" × 3.5" (6 × 9 cm) in dimension to be an official ATC. The next two projects allow you to use some of your art papers to create artist trading cards. Once you've made some ATCs, head to the Share Your Joy Facebook page (link on page 119) to arrange trades with fellow readers!

Shareable Project #3:
Polka Dot Artist Trading Cards

These artist trading cards are a twist on some that I made for a past trade. I used small scraps of art papers left over from my 100 Days Project and punched circles out of them. This gave me a beautiful selection of colorful "dots" to add to a brightly colored ATC background.

Gather Your Supplies

Substrate: watercolor paper or precut ATC cards made of watercolor paper

Collage materials: art papers or scraps of your art papers (colorful art papers are the best option, so try AP1, AP2, AP4, and AP5)

Background paint: fluid acrylic, vibrant acrylic ink, or high-flow acrylic paint

Other: paper trimmer (or pencil, ruler, and scissors), small dishes or watercolor paint palette with wells, pipette, water jar for rinsing brush and diluting paints, square paintbrush (I used a ¾-inch [2 cm] wash), round hole punches (see Tip) in various sizes (⅝ inch [16 mm] maximum), matte medium and brush, glue stick

TIP

I love having various hole punches to add punched shapes and the punched-out paper to my mixed-media art projects. They are not that pricey and are readily available on the market (see Resources, page 118). If you do not have a variety of circle hole punches, you can use just one, such as a small one that you use to create tags, or a three-hole punch. Gluing these punch-outs to the card backgrounds is going to be difficult, so I recommend using some craft tweezers to minimize frustration.

STEP 1

If you are cutting your own ATC bases and not using precut cards, use a paper trimmer (or a ruler, pencil, and scissors) to cut watercolor paper into cards measuring 2.5" × 3.5" (6 × 9 cm). This is the official size for artist trading cards.

STEP 2

Dispense a small amount of fluid acrylic, acrylic ink, or high-flow acrylic paint into a few small dishes or a watercolor paint palette with wells. Three or four colors should be plenty. Dilute the paints by adding water with a pipette, or load your brush with water a few times and add it to the paints. Using a wet brush, apply one color per ATC base. With a bright solid background, the colors of the dots will pop! Cover as many ATC bases as you like and make a variety of different colored backgrounds.

STEP 3

While the ATC backgrounds are drying, punch out circles from some of your art papers. I used three different hole punches—a ¼ inch ([6 mm] standard size), a ½ inch (12 mm), and a ⅝ inch (16 mm). Some hole punches don't work very well on thinner paper, so to avoid frustration, fold thinner papers and punch through two layers. Sort and arrange the cut circles by size and color. Once they're sorted, you'll spend a lot less time searching for the dot you want!

STEP 4

Using a brush, apply matte medium to the upper third of one of your colored card bases (see Tip on the opposite page). Place several dots in different colors and sizes on top of the adhesive. Place some dots off the edge of the card so that the pattern of dots flows nicely over your ATC. Brush a thin layer of matte medium over the dots. You can use the brush to press the dots into the card base. If the dots don't seem to be sticking, press a little harder with the brush. If you are using little dots, you can use the other end of your glue brush to press the dot. When you brush matte medium over the top of the watercolor paper dots, the glue will activate the watercolor and smear it. If this happens, rinse your brush so that you don't stain your matte medium and brush watercolor over the background or other dots!

STEP 5

Repeat the process in step 4 to cover the next third of the card base with dots; repeat again to finish covering the card base. Let the glue dry completely, and trim any overhanging dots so they're flush to the edge. Create as many ATCs as you want for your series. You can follow a multicolored or monochromatic approach, or use one size of dot instead of a variety of sizes to create different looks.

STEP 6

Use the glue stick to adhere backs to your ATCs so they have all the information your trader will need to know. Traditionally, an ATC back lists the fact that it is an artist trading card, the artist's name, the date it was created, where the artist is from, its number in the series and how many cards in the series, its title, and any contact information the artist wants to include (such as email address or social media handle).

Artist Trading Card
Artist: Sarah Gardner
Date created: 9-2022
Place: Cardiff CA
No. 1 of 10
Title: Polka 1

Artist Trading Card
Artist: Sarah Gardner
Date created: 9-2022
Place: Cardiff CA
No. 2 of 10
Title: Polka 2
IG: @juicy.s.art

ATC Backs

Included in one of the pullouts (page 123) is an ATC back you can copy. Print it out and glue it to the back of the ATC, or just write on the blank back of the ATC.

SHAREABLE ART

Shareable Project #4:

Woven Paper Artist Trading Cards

For one of Hanna's swaps in 2015, I made postcards using this method. Weaving is fun and meditative. It is so rewarding to see how each woven card evolves and comes together, transforming strips of paper into a multicolored tapestry. Here, you'll learn a couple of weaving terms and play with some of your pretty art papers as you create some beautiful woven ATCs.

Gather Your Supplies

Substrate: precut ATC cards made of watercolor paper

Weaving materials: art papers (virtually all the art papers could be used for this project), scrapbooking papers, or other collected colorful papers

Other: paper trimmer, scissors, double-sided tape (½ inch [12 mm] wide), fast-drying liquid glue (see Tip), glue stick

TIP

I use a product called Art Glitter Glue, which has a fine nozzle for adding dots of glue. It dries quickly. It is a runny glue, however, so you'll have to take care not to add too much glue to your weaving. You only need a dot.

STEP 1

Cut some of your papers into thin strips, at least ⅛ inch (3 mm) wide and at most ½ inch (12 mm) wide. The length should be at least 4.5 inches (11 cm), but if you're cutting from sheets of art papers, this should not be an issue. I used a paper trimmer to cut my strips, but you can use scissors. Try to get the strips as regular/straight as possible.

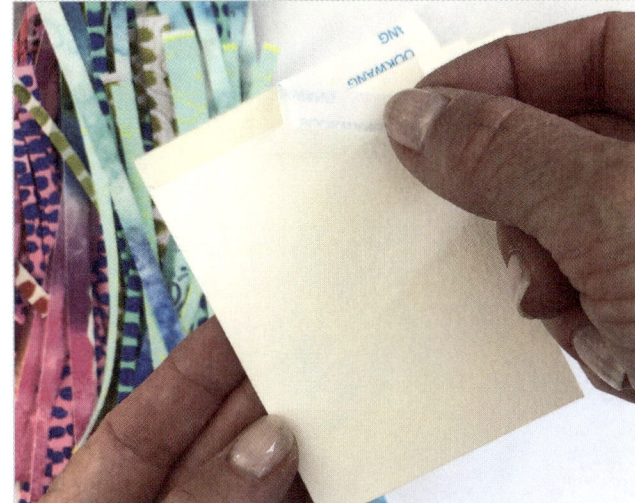

STEP 2

Begin creating the warp, which is the array of threads that are secured in place vertically and through which other yarn is woven to create a weaving. For this project, the warp consists of paper strips secured to an ATC back. At one end of an ATC card base, apply a piece of double-sided tape. It is not necessary to use the whole width of the tape, so secure it with about a third of the width of the tape off the edge of the card. Trim the excess, remove the second peel-off strip, and you are ready to start adding the strips of paper that will form the warp.

STEP 3

Select strips of paper according to your chosen color scheme, and adhere the ends of the strips, nestled next to one another, onto the exposed, sticky side of the tape on the ATC card base. These will need to fit onto the card, so if your last strip is hanging over the edge, trim it with scissors so it is flush with the ATC card base. When your warp is complete, trim any long strips to a more manageable length, about 4.5 inches (11 cm) long.

Here's an example of a card that is all ready for weaving.

STEP 4

Next, start the weft. The "weft" is the thread or yarn that is woven horizontally—over/under and under/over—through the warp. Usually, the yarn wraps around the ends of the warp, but because you are weaving paper strips, you will add a new strip of paper instead of wrapping. To begin, select one strip of paper, and thread it under the first strip in the warp. Then lay it over the next strip in the warp, and continue the pattern until you are at the end of the warp. Depending on how many strips you have in your warp, the weft strip may be over or under the last strip in the warp.

STEP 5

Because you are not wrapping around the ends of the warp, you need to secure the ends of the weft strips. In this example, since my first weft strip is under the warp strips on each side, I place a dot of glue on top of the weft strip. Then I press the two warp strips into the glue dot to adhere it and secure the first strip of weaving. Do this to each weft strip and your weaving will be secure both while you weave and when you're done.

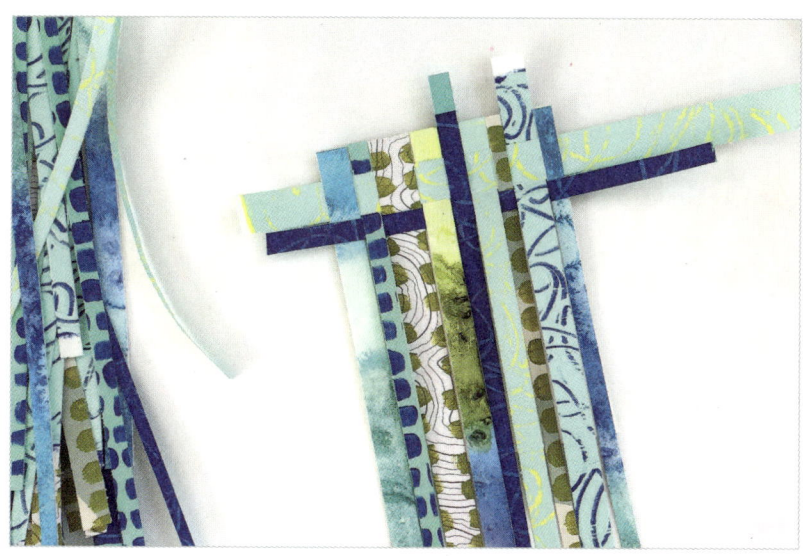

STEP 6

As you work, you will need to alternate how you start the weave. Since the first strip started under the first warp strip, the next weft strip in my ATC will have to start by going over the first warp strip.

STEP 7

Each time you add a weft strip, push it as closely as possible up against the prior weft strip to create a tight weave. Gently pull on any of the warp strips that seem to loosen as you push the weft strip up.

STEP 8

Once you've woven in enough weft strips to cover the ATC card base, glue the ends of the last strip, and then glue each of the top warp strips to the last weft strip by adding a dot to the weft strip.

STEP 9

To finish, lift the woven piece up and away (as far as you can) from the ATC card base, and apply some glue to the middle of the card base. If the weave is stuck in place already, apply glue in whatever space on the card base you can expose. Place a line of glue at the bottom edge as well. Then replace the weave and press to adhere it to the card base. Let the glue dry completely, and then trim the strips overhanging the card edge. Add an ATC back (see Polka Dot Artist Trading Cards step 6, page 66).

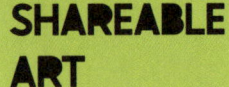
Shareable Project #5:

Watercolor Rainbow Greeting Card

In mixed media, watercolor is a versatile medium that you can use for layered backgrounds or to add hints of sheer color and create colorful focal-point ephemera. We do all three in this project. This greeting card can be used as a lovely birthday card, friendship greeting, or even a thank-you note.

Gather Your Supplies

Substrate: watercolor paper or heavy card stock (at least 184 lb/300 gsm), or precut and folded cards (see Tip), lightweight watercolor or mixed-media paper (about 80 lb/119 gsm)

Background collage materials: vintage book text or dictionary text, sheet music, ledger paper with writing/typing, or other printed/written text

Background media: absorbent ground or gesso (thinned with water), watercolors (pan or fluid), white gouache, pink and yellow watercolors

Rainbow ephemera supplies: set of watercolors with all the colors of the rainbow (including iridescent colors if you have them), gold acrylic ink (I use Dr. Ph. Martin's Iridescent Calligraphy Colors in copper plate gold)

Tools: acrylic paintbrush (¾-inch [2 cm] wash), watercolor paintbrushes (round #4, round #6, and round #0), watercolor palette with wells, drinking straw

Optional: printed words or phrases to add to the front and/or inside of the card

Other: paper trimmer (or pencil, ruler, and scissors), pencil, ruler, bone folder, glue stick, water jar

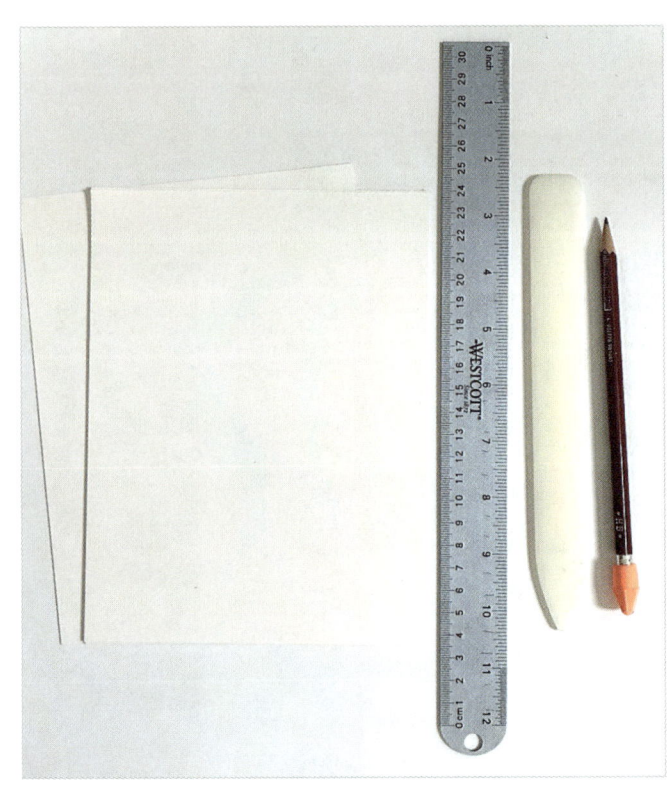

STEP 1

If you are cutting and folding your own cards, I suggest a card that is at least 4" × 6" (10 × 15 cm) when folded. To create a card this size, cut your substrate to 8" × 6" (20 × 15 cm) using a paper trimmer (or a ruler, pencil, and scissors). You want to be as accurate as possible so that your card folds nicely. Use a ruler and pencil to mark the center at 4 inches (10 cm). Then hold the ruler at this mark, even with both edges of the paper. Use the pointed end of the bone folder to score a line against the edge of the ruler, making sure that the score line is at the 4-inch (10 cm) point.

Fold the card at the score line, away from the scoring. Use the side of the bone folder to burnish the fold. Erase the pencil marks from the fold.

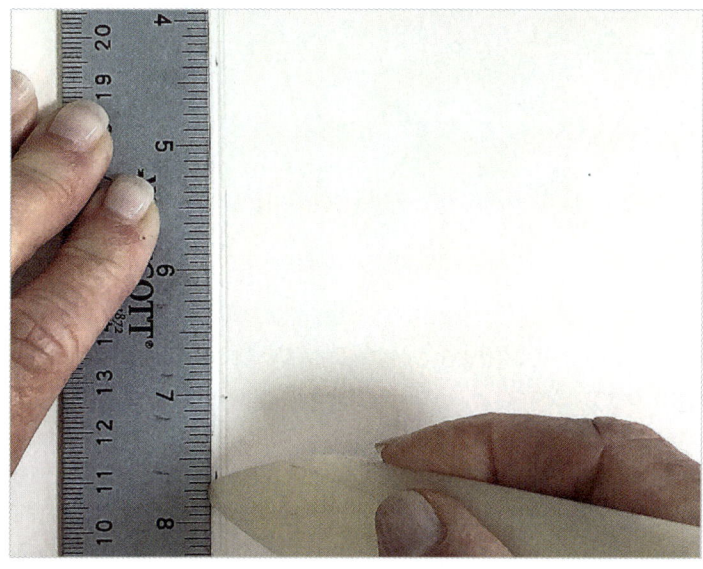

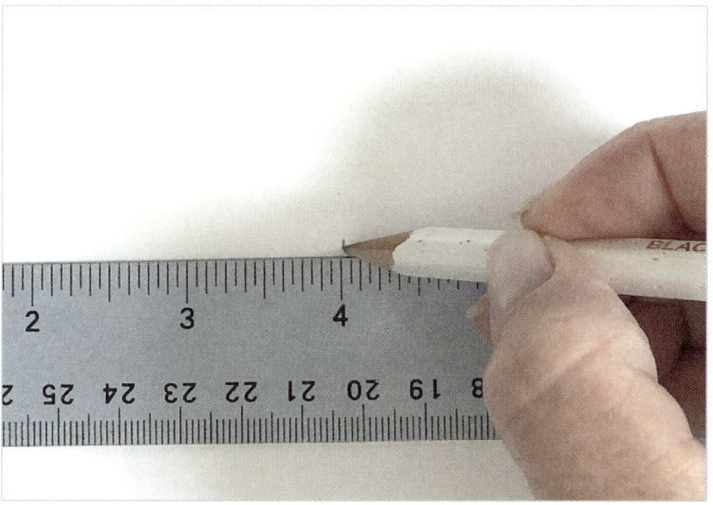

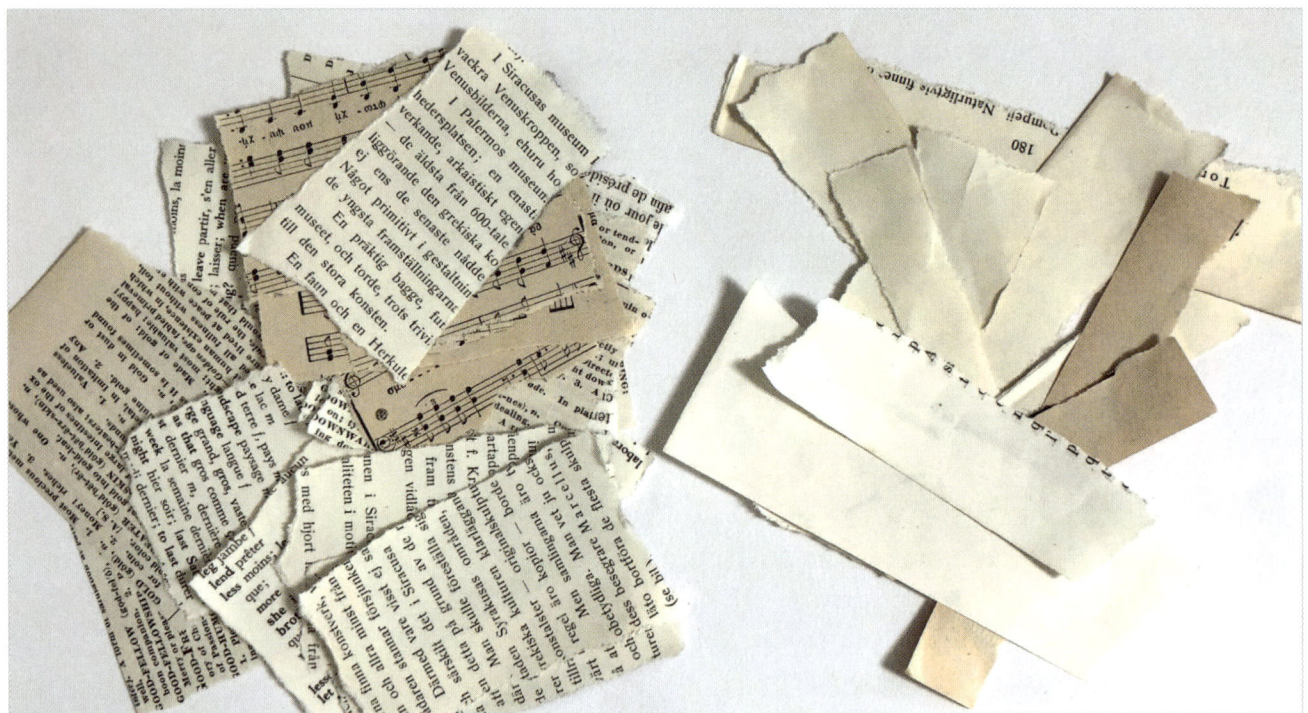

STEP 2

Gather together the book text and other papers that you have, and tear some of them into pieces, approximately 1 to 2 inches (2.5 to 5 cm) on all sides. If some of your book text has margins, cut these off. You want text to show up in your collage background, and every bit of space on the front of the card counts! Vintage book paper is aged and usually of decent quality, so I save these margin pieces to add written or stamped words or phrases. Then I adhere them to my cards, art journal, or other projects.

STEP 3

Unfold a card, and place it on your work surface, outside up, back at the top and front at the bottom. Collage pieces of the book text to cover the entire card front. It should look a little like patchwork, with collage pieces overlapping each other. With scissors, trim the pieces that will bump up against the fold in the card so they will be flush with the fold. It's okay if some pieces overhang the edges of the card. Let the glue dry completely, and then trim the collage to be flush with the card edges before you move on to step 4.

STEP 4

With an acrylic paintbrush (I used a ¾-inch [2 cm] wash), apply a thin layer of absorbent ground or diluted gesso (to make it more transparent) to the collage layer, covering it completely. Let this dry before moving on to step 5.

STEP 5

Dispense several shades of blue watercolor into a palette with wells. If you're using watercolors from a tube, a very small amount goes a long way when you add water. If you are using liquid watercolor, dispense a small amount and avoid diluting it too much with water. With a wet round watercolor brush (I used a round #6), pick up one of the blues, and add it in puddles to the dry surface of the prepared card front. If it is dark and you cannot see the book text through it, add a little water to your brush, and then apply the wet brush to the color on the card to dilute it a little. Let this layer dry completely before adding the next layer of color.

STEP 6

Clean the brush, and then dip it into your water jar to pick up some water. Apply water to a small area of the card not yet covered in color. You can reactivate the first color a little at the edges as you do this. Then, before the water dries, add a different blue to your brush and drop color with your brush tip into the watery areas you just added to the card. Watch as the color flows into the water. Let this layer of color dry completely before going on to step 7.

STEP 7

With a wet brush and a third blue, apply some saturated color in one or two puddles, as you did in step 6. Then, before this paint dries, use a straw to blow the watery color into tendrils and sprays over the card. If there are still areas of the card front that don't have color, you can create more puddles and blow them into tendrils, or add a little color to your brush and apply this to these areas. Let this layer dry overnight so there's less chance of the gouache in step 8 reactivating the blue watercolors.

STEP 8

Dispense a small amount of white gouache into a well of the paint palette. Wet a brush (I used a round #4), and pick up a little of the white paint. Apply it to the card in about three distinct "clouds." You can use circular motions with the brush to give the clouds a fluffy look. Use less water with this application than you did with the blues. If the clouds reactivate the blues below them and fade, wait until the first layer of gouache is dry and then add another layer of white over the clouds. Use a little less water for this layer. If they still seem to fade, wait for a longer period of time for everything to dry thoroughly, and then add a final layer of white gouache. Let the white paint dry before moving to step 9.

STEP 9

Dispense a small amount of yellow and a little pink into two other wells of the palette. (I used bismuth vanadate yellow by Daniel Smith and shell pink by Holbein). One at a time, add some water to the wells in the palette with the yellow and pink paints. With a clean, damp brush, pick up some of the watery pink paint and apply small amounts of it to the clouds of white paint, adding a little dimension to the clouds at the tops and inside them. Add a little of the yellow at the bottom of each cloud. When applying these colors to your clouds, start with very small amounts of color and add more, if needed. You don't want to overdo it and end up with pink/yellow/orange clouds. You want to see some of the white. While your colored clouds dry, move on to step 10.

STEP 10

For a focal point for the front of the card, make some rainbows using a lightweight sheet of watercolor or mixed-media paper and a set of colorful watercolors. First, wet a watercolor brush (a round #0 or #1), and dip it into one color of paint. Create a little puddle of this color on your paint palette lid. Create a small arch on your paper using this paint. Dispense some gold ink into a well of your paint palette. With a slightly damp brush, pick up some of the gold paint and create the second arch of the rainbow following the shape of the first arch (see Tip below). Rinse your brush and pick up a new color of watercolor paint for the third arch. Finally, with a clean brush, use a different color of watercolor to create the last arch of your rainbow.

TIP

I like to add the "gold" ink at either the second or third arch so that other colors kind of enclose it, or frame it, within the rainbow. I found that if I use the gold as the first or final arch, the ink doesn't stand out as well as a color would, so the rainbow doesn't pop.

STEP 11

Make several rainbows and mix up your color combinations. Use little brush marks when you first start to form the arch versus trying to make an arch in one stroke. Then, you can go back and thicken the arch to match the prior arch in size. Leave a small amount of white space between each arch.

STEP 12

When your rainbows are dry, cut them out to use as focal points in your cards. (If you don't end up liking a few, you don't need to use them.) I like to leave a small amount of white paper as a border around my rainbows. Fussy-cutting like this takes practice and patience, so take your time.

STEP 13

Optional: Create some words or phrases to use on the front or inside of your cards. I used some of the margin scraps from the book text collage I used earlier and a pen and some letter stamps to create words. Using a glue stick, adhere a rainbow to each of the cloudy card backgrounds. Placement off to one side versus in the center of the card is more pleasing to the eye. Add a sentiment to the front, or you can add a greeting to the inside of the card. And you always have the option of leaving words out so that you can use the card for any occasion. Match your cards with envelopes and store them with your stationery. Or tie a ribbon around the set, and give all the cards as a gift to someone else!

Shareable Project #6:
Abstract Collage Note Card

Collage is a very meditative process for me. It's a bit like putting a puzzle together, but without any pressure to create a specific result. Abstract collage is about color and contrast, balance and proportion, concepts that call upon your observation and attention. And abstract collage is fun because you can follow your intuition and just play—you're not trying to create anything representational.

Gather Your Supplies

Substrate: watercolor paper or heavy card stock (at least 184 lb/300 gsm) or precut and folded cards

Collage materials: art papers (virtually all the art papers could be used for this project), vintage book text, sheet music, metallic embellished or printed tissue paper

Optional: watercolor ephemera (step-by-step included), printed words or phrases to add to the front and/or inside, lightweight watercolor or medium-weight mixed-media paper, watercolors, round #0 watercolor brush, water jar, paper towel

Other: glue stick, pencil, ruler, and scissors, bone folder*

STEP 1

To begin choosing your collage papers, it is helpful to select one of your more colorful and intricate art papers as a starting point. Include some high-contrast (black-and-white) pieces and some neutral (such as vintage book text or sheet music). Tear your collage materials to about 3" × 3" (8 × 8 cm) in size before beginning to make the process flow more smoothly. You can tear them down further as you work. Working on the front of the card (I'm using purchased cards with envelopes from Strathmore), start by laying collage pieces down to "audition" placement of different colors, sizes, and types of papers. Leave a rough border of about ¼ to ½ inch (6 to 13 mm) around the edges of your collage to frame it on the front of the card.

TIP

As an easy rule of thumb, add dark and light pieces in a composition that is in a ratio of about one-third to two-thirds. This is the "rule of thirds." It means, for example, that if you cover the card front with mostly light pieces, the remaining third of the composition should be dark.

Another trick is to picture a horizon through a section of the collage to create separate blocks of content separated by this line. It's a familiar composition because we see the horizon every day. When we see this represented in art, we respond positively. If you use the rule of thirds, you can have either one-third "sky" and two-thirds "earth" or vice versa. The sky can consist of lighter collage pieces, and the earth can be darker papers.

STEP 2

Once you have everything where you want it, take a picture with your phone to aid you as you glue down the pieces. Pieces underneath others will have to be glued down first, and you'll have to remove the pieces on top, so it helps to have the photograph as a reminder.

TIP

I usually use an old catalog to apply glue to the backs of my collage pieces. I place the collage piece right-side down on a page of the catalog and apply glue to the wrong side. Glue goes off the edge onto the catalog page. I lay my next piece down on a clean area of the catalog and continue until the page has too much glue on it to be helpful; then I turn to a fresh page of the catalog and continue gluing.

STEP 3

Once the collage is glued in place, you have the option of adding a focal point to the front of the card. I arranged shapes on top of the collage where they looked pleasing and glued them down. If you've worked in a horizon on your collage, the line where the "earth" and "sky" meet is a good placement for a focal point.

The finished collages are quite lovely!

Creating Watercolor Ephemera

Another option for focal points is to create some ephemera that goes with the colors in your collage(s). Scan the QR code to see how I made some watercolor botanical stems to add as focal points. Once dry, fussy-cut the botanical and add a stem to the front of your cards.

STEP 1

Use a piece of lightweight watercolor paper or medium-weight mixed-media paper (both can withstand wet media), a round #0 watercolor brush, and watercolors that coordinate with your collage(s). Wet the brush and tap it on the rim of your water jar to remove excess water. Pick up a neutral tone, like a gold or brown, and add the watery color to your paint palette so that the paint is watered down and a bit lighter.

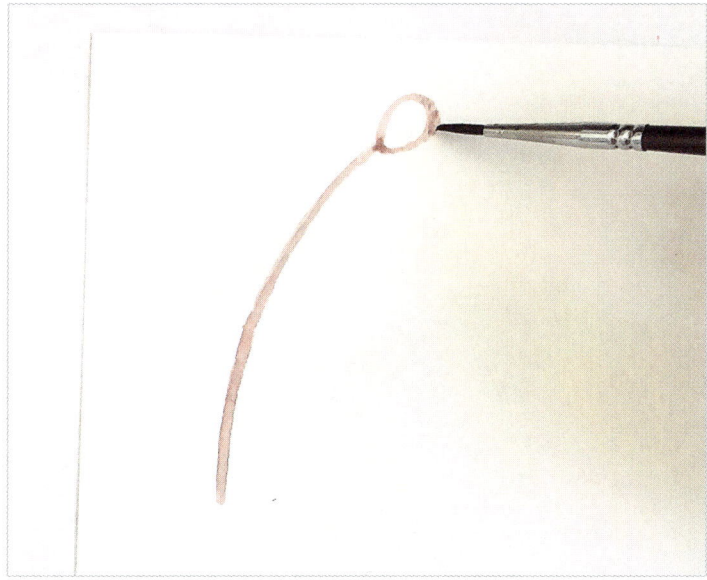

STEP 2

Using the very end of the brush tip, create a slightly arched line (bowing either right or left), then add a loop or drop-shaped leaf at the top of the line. Before the paint dries, pick up some water on your brush and paint within the leaf shape with slightly tinted water.

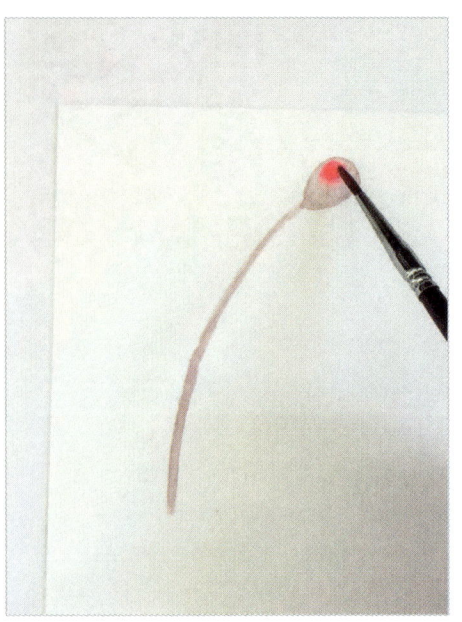

STEP 3

Pick up a small amount of paint in a color you feel will complement your collage and add it to the watery leaf shape by touching it to the water within the shape. The paint will spread out.

STEP 4

Using the watery neutral you started with, create two more drop-shaped leaves below the top leaf on each side of the stem. Fill these both with water and repeat the process in step 3. Continue repeating this process all the way down the stem.

STEP 5

Create several of these stems in different colors that go with your collages. Once they are completely dry, fussy-cut them out. You can use a craft knife to cut out openings between the leaves that are touching if you have difficulty getting your scissors into these areas.

Real Art Connections: A Conversation about Sharing Joy with Jana Clinard-Harris

I "met" Jana quite a few years ago when we both participated in iHanna's DIY Postcard Swap. We've exchanged a couple of postcards this way over the years. But since we've both been active on Instagram, we've become friends and have exchanged other art with each other. Jana and I share the view that social media is a way for us to share our joy. With this focus, we are not as trapped in the competition and comparison that sometimes feels dominant there. Jana's artwork can most certainly be called joyful. When we talked, she told me how creating gives her joy and how sharing her art is part of making her own positive impact on the world. Combining the connections of our virtual art community with the real-life sharing of art is something we have both been doing—and getting joy out of—for quite a while. We hope that this conversation will encourage and inspire you to share your creativity in similar ways.

S: How did you come to start sharing your art in the ways that you do?

J: It's kind of two-fold. Just like you, the iHanna DIY Postcard Swap was the beginning of it all. Right before I did my first iHanna swap, I had just gotten back into making art and making art a priority. In 2018, I received some health diagnoses that were life-changing for me. It made me look at my life differently. And it was, for me, a voice in my head wondering, "What are you leaving behind? What are you contributing to the world? What will your kids look back on and see?" A central focus of my life, which might be shorter now, became a desire to make a mark and leave something positive behind when I'm gone. So this spurred me into making art daily.

S: You have another Instagram called @janasharesjoy, right?

J: Yes. I started that in the pandemic. We were all struggling so much, and there was so much negativity out there, and everyone's mental health was really suffering. I could see this. Initially, I started @janasharesjoy because I wanted to share other artists' work. I thought everyone could use some encouragement. It's been really positive. The feedback that I get is, "I needed this today!" That's the whole reason I'm doing this. It's worth it to do.

S: I see that. You feel that sense of making a difference and feeling connected to other artists. Part of my motivation for sharing my art is to pay it forward somehow. "Pay it forward" is kind of my default! To me, you put it out there, you share it, you give it away with no expectation of any reciprocity. But because it's a positive thing, that's positive energy you're putting out into the world, and it's increasing positivity and joy in a kind of ripple effect.

J: Right. I wasn't putting art on Facebook, so this was like the first foray into sharing my art like this. That's why I went beyond social media and started mailing art to people. My purpose was to put my art out in the world and just get back to being creative. So I think the postcard swap along with this press for a sense of what I was leaving in the world combined to become a habit of physically giving my art to people who would feel a connection to it. I started asking followers on Instagram to send me the names of anyone they thought could use a little boost or art mail to raise their spirits. So that's my whole purpose: just giving away my art to people who will enjoy it.

S: I see that. This comes through clearly on your Instagram accounts.

J: This sense of purpose guides how I use Instagram now. I really spend a lot of time responding to people. I try really hard not to just scroll and look at posts but to read captions. Because so many times, you'll read into it and get past those first couple sentences, and you'll find a struggle or someone who needs a

little encouragement. It can make a difference in someone's day—life even.

S: You're approaching social media in a way that makes it meaningful. The combination of social media connections with our art community and the sharing of our art by mailing it to someone in that community forms a rewarding connection. It adds another dimension to that positive feeling that we want to generate on social media.

J: Absolutely. This art community on Instagram, these are my friends. I honestly couldn't do without this connection now. The support I've gotten and give back is meaningful and real, so it makes these connections real for me.

S: It's sharing creativity and sharing joy. And when you're putting that out into the world, I believe it has a positive impact. What is it that you tend to share most often when you are sending art away to people?

J: Mostly what I send are my 4-by-6 collages. I started with that postcard format, and it continued because it's a good size—easy to make and easy to send in the mail. I don't go larger very often at all. I may make a zine or, on a rare occasion, a panel that someone could hang on the wall. But the 4-by-6 collages can be put in a standard frame, put up on a bulletin board, or put in someone's journal. I try to make things that people will find a connection with. And themes of nature, children, flowers, birds, and butterflies connect pretty universally with all of us.

S: Your collages are so whimsical, colorful, and happy. I think you've said that this "place" you collage onto your cards is like a world you can escape to. So while you're creating, you're there experiencing joy, but the collage you're creating represents joy as well.

J: Yes. That's true. It's an escape, maybe a little fantasy world where everything is positive and the burdens of daily life don't exist.

S: It gives your work more meaning, and it really brightens someone's day when they get it in the mail!

J: Yes, it does. And another thing I do is when I'm sending someone something—I have their name and Instagram handle—I look at their account to see what they like. And if someone else has sent me their name, I ask them, "What do they like . . . do they have pets, kids?" I want to send them something they can connect with, not just a pretty piece of art.

S: That's amazing. And that is what makes what you are doing so special, I think. I love your collages. The images and colors you use are happy and playful, kind of reminders of simpler things that hold so much joy for us when we notice them. I love your line-drawn botanicals and of course how you use a palette knife to add one or two daubs of bright acrylic paint as a finishing touch! I dubbed this "Jana's Icing" when I used this technique to finish collages I made for the Index Card a Day challenge in 2021, remember?

J: I love that so much! #janasicing! My collages really are another world that I visit as I'm creating. That's where I want to be.

S: Do you have any advice for readers who want to share their art?

J: People are so afraid to share. But they should know that I've never run across anybody who shared their work and regretted it. Most often, it's followers offering encouragement. We want everyone to keep trying, making, and sharing. Any positive thing you put out into the world is going to make all of us happier and the world a better place.

S: We all second-guess ourselves. We all start out as beginners.

J: It's never going to be as bad as you think in your mind! That's just not going to happen. I've never experienced it in the creative community.

S: And comparison is another thing that can discourage people. It's so true that comparison is the thief of joy!

J: Take the comparison and turn it around. You can change "comparison" to "inspiration." It's a matter of your mindset.

S: Yes! I'm inspired all the time by what people share. Instead of comparing your work or your level to anyone else's, take it in, be inspired by it. There's room for everyone's style out there. And whatever you make will be part of you and totally unique to you. There's no comparison for that.

Shareable Project #7:

Valentine Paper Mobile

These paper mobiles are something we made at Girls' ARTisan Camp, and then I converted it to a Valentine's Day Art Play Date. For my 100 Days Project in 2021, I made one hundred paper mobiles. The 100 Days Project usually starts up in February, so I made quite a few heart mobiles for the project. You can easily gather this paper mobile up into a stack of hearts, put it into an envelope, and mail. Your Valentine will surely cherish it!

Gather Your Supplies

Heart shapes template (page 125)

Substrates: one heavy card stock or watercolor art paper for one side of the mobile shapes and different (any weight) papers for the other side (I recommend AP6 for the heavy weight paper and any of the papers from AP1, AP2, AP4, AP5, and AP8 for the lightweight) and/or purchased scrapbooking paper or other printed paper

Other: scissors, glue stick, pencil, cotton cord or thick string or yarn, one color of acrylic paint to "paint" the mobile cord, small precision scissors

Embellishing items: smaller cutout hearts from art papers, washi tape, pens, heart-shaped hole punches, water-soluble crayons, small brush , words to glue onto the front of each mobile shape (see pullout on page 125)

STEP 1

Tear out the heart pullout on page 125, or copy it onto card stock using your printer. Then cut out all the hearts. You'll use them to trace mirror images onto paper that will stick together closely when they are cut out. Before starting to trace the hearts onto your art papers, mark one side of the template with "1" and the other side with "2." Trace around each of the hearts you are using onto the heavy card stock or watercolor art papers with the "1" facing up toward you. Then, turn all of the heart templates over and trace onto lighter-weight papers you choose with the "2" facing up toward you. I traced the side 2 onto several different papers, including one heart from scrapbooking paper. This way, you will have mirror-image hearts that will be flush at the edge when you glue them, back to back, around the string to create the chain of hearts for your mobile.

STEP 2

Match up the hearts and decide which order to glue them together around a string. I usually go from big to small. Set the paired hearts aside. Measure and cut a length of cord or string that is about 1.5 yards (1.5 meters) long. Determine the dominant color in the papers, and choose an acrylic paint color that closely matches. Place the string on a piece of scrap paper, and use a brush to paint it, making sure to cover the entire string. Let dry completely before moving on to step 3.

STEP 3

Gather the painted string, the cutout hearts, and a glue stick, and begin assembling your mobile. Beginning with the two top heart shapes, generously apply glue to the back side of both shapes. Create a loop at one end of the string, and place the two ends of the loop at the center of one of the glued hearts. Pull the long end of the string down toward the bottom of the first heart shape, and then place the other glued heart glue-side down on top of the string and the heart. Press firmly so that the string gets stuck to the glue and stays put and the two heart shapes are securely stuck together. Match the edges of the hearts as closely as possible. This way the end of the string that forms the loop will be glued in between the two heart shapes, and the string that continues from the bottom of this heart is ready for the next heart in the chain.

STEP 4

Approximately 1.5 to 2 inches (4 to 5 cm) below the bottom of the first heart on the string, repeat the gluing process in step 3 for the next heart in the chain. Repeat this process for all the hearts you want to add to your mobile. Once all the hearts are glued together around the string, let the glue dry. Cut any excess string. Trim any mismatched edges with scissors.

STEP 5

Now, it's time to embellish your Valentine mobile! The pullout has some words and phrases you can use. Choose what you want your mobile to say. You may even want to write out some words and then cut these out to use on your mobile. Preprinted scrapbooking ephemera words are plentiful in the marketplace as well. If you have a heart hole punch, you can punch out little hearts to add to your big hearts. I punched shiny hearts out of some metallic scrapbooking paper. You can cut more hearts out of your art papers to layer onto the hearts of the mobile as well. You can use the templates to cut these.

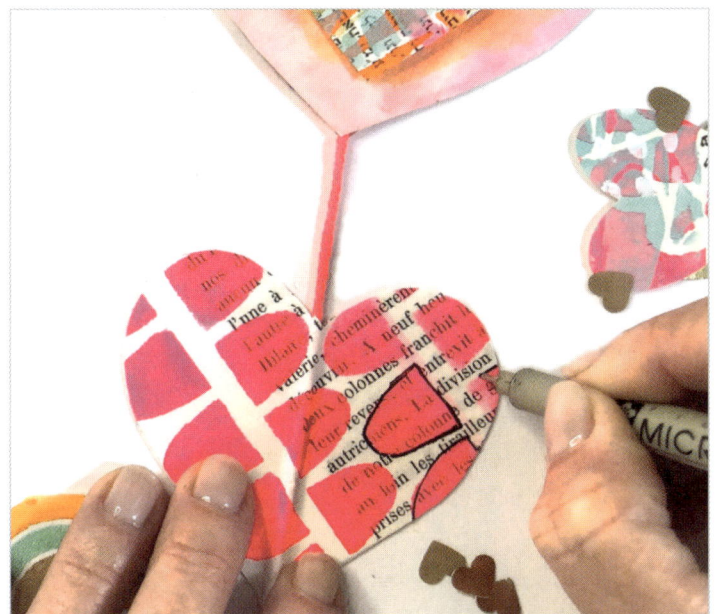

STEP 6

Use a pen to outline shapes on the art papers. I used black ink for contrast, knowing that the words I'm adding will be black type.

STEP 7

I cut out some smaller hearts to add some of the plain(ish) watercolor heart shapes in my mobile. Punched hearts from metallic gold paper add a shiny touch. I used one of my watercolor rainbows too! And I framed some of my words with washi tape.

I used an X-Acto knife to make a cutout in one of my hearts and added some transparent plastic behind it with a little glue. Then I put in a few of my tiny foil hearts and glued the edges of this to create a little shaker heart.

STEP 8

I always like to try to integrate cutout words into the backgrounds of my mixed-media projects. There are many ways to do this. Here, I outlined the word *shine* with the same black pen I had used to outline the shapes in the heart. The other method I often use is to colorize the white paper of the word using a water-soluble crayon and a little water. To do this, mark up the word with the crayon of your choice. Then use a slightly wet brush to activate the crayon and colorize the paper.

I think one of the reasons my mobile turned out so well is that I used a cohesive and consistent color palette in creating all my art papers. It was not difficult to choose papers that went together, and I was even inspired by the scrapbooking paper with little suns on it to create a cute saying on one side of my mobile. I would love to see yours if you make one! Please tag me on Instagram—@juicy.s.art!

Shareable Project #8:

Intention Journals

A small, handmade journal is a wonderful place to keep important thoughts and memories, embellished with art and doodling. Living intentionally is a big part of my art practice. Combining creativity with intention-setting is not only fun but also meaningful. When you create one of these intention journals as a gift for someone else, you give them the gift of your joyful art and an opportunity to experience the joy of using it to live with intention. Here, we'll create two intention journals, one for a friend and one for you. For a flip-through of a finished intention journal, scan the QR code at the end of this shareable project!

Gather Your Supplies

Substrates:

- For the cover: 8.5" × 11" (22 × 28 cm) piece of heavy card stock or watercolor paper (at least 184 lb/300 gsm)—I used a sheet of Watercolor Clouds from Art Paper #6 (page 32)

- For the pages: sulfite paper, scrapbooking paper (lightweight card stock, approximately five different prints and/or solid colors), book text, vintage ledger paper, mulberry paper, various narrow-lined or graph papers cut into small pieces

Supplies and Tools:

- For the cover: fluid matte medium and glue brush, black-and-white printed tissue paper, white gesso and palette knife, off-white and a variety of acrylic paints from your chosen palette, metallic embellished tissue paper, dish or paint palette, stencils and sponge applicators, Stabilo All in black (or a soft graphite pencil), black acrylic ink, paintbrush (round #10), page trimmer (or ruler, pencil, and scissors)

- For the pages: one or two watercolor paint colors (one metallic or iridescent if you have it), watercolor brush (round #10), deckled ruler, acrylic paints in several matching or coordinating colors with your cover, paint-scraping tool (like an old credit card), palette knife, gold or other iridescent acrylic ink

- For binding: bone folder, binder clips, awl, waxed cotton or linen cord, large needle, scissors

- Other: "Intention Journal" labels from the pullout section (page 122), washi tape, corner rounding punch (optional), various scrapbooking or other cut-out images to use as embellishing ephemera

The Cover

We start this shareable project by making the covers of the journals. These covers are true mixed-media artworks because they're full of layers! It is always easier to start any mixed-media project with a page that has something on it already, so I used one of my art papers featuring watercolor clouds. This "substrate" is 8.5" × 11" (22 × 28 cm), so I was able to create two inspiration journal covers measuring 4.25" × 5.5" (11 × 14 cm) when folded.

STEP 1

First, use some fluid matte medium to adhere a few pieces of black-and-white printed tissue paper in random spots over the substrate. Apply a small amount of the adhesive in a thin layer to the substrate, place the tissue over that, and then brush another thin layer of the matte medium on top. The "paper" part of the tissue paper will disappear this way, with only the black-and-white printed detail appearing. Wait for this to dry before moving on to step 2.

STEP 2

Using a palette knife, apply white gesso over the tissue in random areas, not covering the whole substrate. Let this dry before moving on to step 3.

STEP 3

Dispense about five colors of bright acrylic paint into a dish or paint palette. Using your fingers, add these colors to the cover. Try to apply the paint randomly, and group some of the colors/marks together so there isn't a regular pattern to the fingerprints. Wiping your fingers between colors will keep the colors bright and unmixed as you apply them next to one another. It's okay if some of the colors mix slightly as the marks overlap, but try to keep this to a minimum. Let your finger painting dry completely before moving on to step 4.

STEP 4

Tear up some tissue paper with metallic detail into small pieces. Adhere these using fluid matte medium and an inexpensive paintbrush. Do this using the same technique described in step 1. Let this layer dry before moving on to step 5.

STEP 5

Through one of your stencils, sponge off-white paint over the entire cover. For a layer like this, I like to use a stencil that has some medium openings versus very small or very large ones. The tile grid I used is the perfect example. This layer of off-white pushes back some of your bright finger painting and adds dimensional interest. Let this paint dry before going on to step 6.

STEP 6

It's time to add a little grunge. Using a Stabilo All in black or a soft graphite pencil, scribble some lines crisscrossing all over the surface.

STEP 7

Next, create texture using another stencil. This stencil can have smaller openings. Using a palette knife, press a heavy-body acrylic paint through the stencil openings so that the paint is level with the stencil. Use a color that's a bit lighter than all the finger-painting colors. This layer should not cover the whole substrate; you just want some areas that will stand up off the surface a little. When you remove the stencil to create more areas of texture, be careful not to put the stencil on top of the areas you have already created. It will take a while for this paint to dry. Wait until it does before moving on to the final layer.

STEP 8

Using a medium to large round brush (I used a #10), mix a bit of water into a few drops of black acrylic ink. With the brush loaded with ink, tap it over the substrate to create random splatter all over it. This ink must be completely dry before moving on to step 9.

STEP 9

Using a paper trimmer (or a ruler, pencil, and scissors), cut the substrate in half so you have two pieces measuring 5.5" × 8.5" (14 × 22 cm). To finish the covers, glue some vintage ledger or book text to the inside, or reverse side, of the covers. Be sure to apply the glue to the entire surface of the covers, including the edges. Use a bone folder or a scraping tool (like an old credit card) to burnish the paper onto the inside cover to secure it evenly and get all the bubbles out.

STEP 10

Measure the center of the cover at 4.25 inches (11 cm), and mark it with a pencil. Place a ruler just to the side of the mark and use the pointed end of a bone folder to score the center fold. Go over the score several times with the end of the bone folder so that the scoring goes through the thick layer of the covers. Fold the insides together at the score, and then use the bone folder to burnish the fold. I used a corner punch to round the corners of the covers. This step is optional.

The Pages

I selected some scrapbooking papers that would pick up the colors in my cover. I also chose some with some metallic/foil detailing since I have that in my cover too. I chose at least one scrapbooking paper (card stock) that is two-sided (colored on both sides). I also chose a nice green, textured piece of mulberry paper to add variety. To really personalize some of the pages, I like to add lines for journaling or just to add some color to the blank page. So, that's where we start.

STEP 1

Using a large round watercolor brush (I used a #10), create wide lines of color on a sheet of white sulfite paper. I created several options, but I won't use all of these in my journal. I used two of these in my journals.

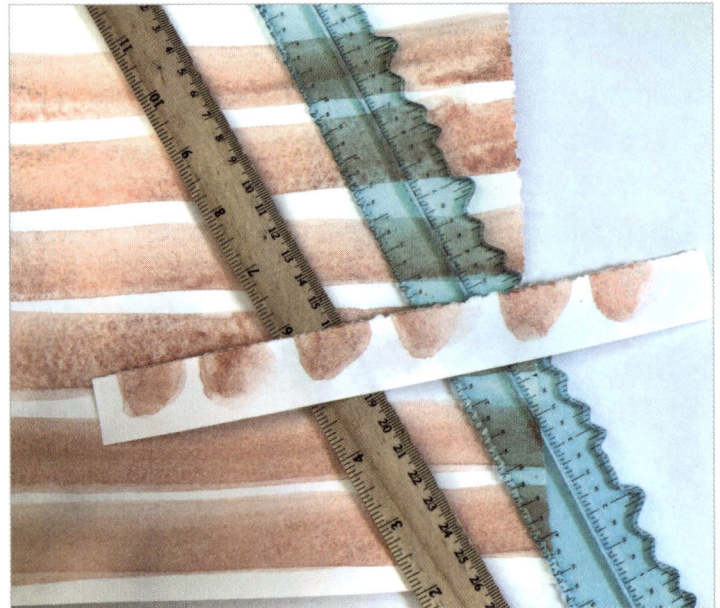

STEP 2

Once the watercolor lines papers are dry, it's time to gather all the papers for the pages and cut them down to size. One way to make it a little interesting is to cut them using a tearing technique with a deckled ruler. (You can buy these from scrapbooking supply vendors, or create your own by distressing a cheap wooden ruler using a wood file, creating notches in the edge.) Here's the main thing to remember: Your pages can vary in size, but none should be more than 5" × 8" (13 × 20 cm). When all the pages are folded and the journal is bound, they should fit nicely inside the covers. I like to cut some pages smaller to add variety, so feel free to get creative in this way! Optional: Create a trifold. One side of the page will be twice as long as the other side, so that the longer side folds in toward the center of the journal. A good rule of thumb here is to cut a piece of scrapbooking paper (usually 12" × 12" [30 × 30 cm]) in thirds. One third is 4" × 12" (10 × 30 cm). The long folded side is therefore 8" × 4" (20 × 10 cm) and the short side is 4" × 4" (10 × 10 cm). You can see this clearly in the flip through video provided as a bonus. Scan the QR code at the end of this project for a link to the video.

STEP 3

Once you have all your pages cut down to the right sizes, separate the papers that are blank on one side, including the watercolor-lined papers you created. Since I created two journals, I had two sets of pages. To add color to the plain backs of these papers, add paint as follows: (A) Apply small drops of two colors of paint to the back of the pages. Then use a scraping tool to spread and mix the paints right on the pages. Cover the pages completely this way. (B) Use white and two other analogous colors, and use a paintbrush to mix the paints in a mottled, variegated finish all over the pages. (C) Simply paint the back of the pages with one color of acrylic paint.

(D) Use an off-white and one other color of acrylic paint, and mix slightly with a palette knife. Apply the paint to the blank page with the palette knife, scraping and spreading to cover the pages completely. Once dry, drop gold or other metallic acrylic ink onto the pages. Smoosh two painted pages together to get the ink to spread randomly onto to both pages. (E) Paint the pages a solid, darker color using a rough, bristly brush. Then, using a palette knife, scrape an off-white or much lighter paint over the first paint layer in a random manner. Make sure all painted pages are completely dry before moving to the book binding process.

STEP 4

Fold each piece of paper in half. If you are making any trifold pages, fold those in thirds. Then arrange all the pages in a way that you find pleasing by stacking them and nestling them together at the fold. When you have them arranged the way you like, set all the folded pages into the center fold of the cover, and use a binder clip to hold everything together

STEP 5

You can add "journal blocks"—cut pieces of lined and other writing papers—and other ephemera before you bind the journal or afterward. Cut down the various lined and graph papers so they fit nicely onto the pages of the journal. You can use a corner punch to round the corners of some of these if you like. Adhere these journaling blocks to the pages with a glue stick or use some washi tape to stick them to other pages. Adhere the label provided in the pullout section (page 123) to the inside front cover. Then add decorative ephemera to some of the pages.

Binding the Journals

Bookbinding is a whole world in and of itself. There are so many fancy ways to bind a book, but here we're just using a basic pamphlet stitch.

STEP 1

Make sure that the center folds are aligned and snug against the cover. Clip this together so that everything stays in place as you bind the journal. To do a basic pamphlet stitch, use an awl to create three holes in the spine of the journal: one at the center and two more on either side, approximately 1 inch (2.5 cm) from the center hole.

STEP 2

Thread a large needle with 2 to 3 feet (60 to 90 cm) of waxed linen or waxed cotton cord. You can use any yarn or string that you like, but waxed linen is fairly standard for bookbinding.

STEP 3

From the inside of the spine, pull the needle and cord through the center hole to the outer spine of the journal. Pull it all the way through, leaving about 4 to 5 inches (10 to 13 cm) of cord trailing out of the hole inside the journal. Hold this "tail" with the thumb of the hand holding the journal.

STEP 4

Now pull the needle and cord through one of the other holes, all the way into the center fold, creating a "stitch" between the two holes on the spine of the journal.

STEP 5

Next, pull the needle and cord through the remaining hole from the center fold to the outside spine. Pull it tightly so that there is no slack in the big "stitch" running from one hole to the other along the center fold.

STEP 6

Finally, pull the needle and cord back through the center hole and into the center fold. Pull the cord all the way through to create the final "stitch" on the spine of the journal.

STEP 7

Now you should have both the "tail" you left at the beginning and the needle end of the cord coming through the center hole. Pull the tail to one side of the center "stitch" and the needle end (remove the needle) to the other side of the center stitch. Tie a square knot around the center stitch and trim the cord to a length that you like.

STEP 8

Add a closure. A simple piece of ribbon or torn strip of fabric a bit longer than 3 feet (1 m) will wrap around nicely, and you can tie a bow!

Shareable Project #9:

Embellished Envelopes

Just seeing an embellished envelope among junk mail and billing statements is enough to bring joy! A pretty painted envelope foretells the artful contents inside. I decorate envelopes like this to mail my Etsy orders out. I usually only embellish one side of an envelope, but feel free to decorate both if you are so inclined.

Gather Your Supplies

Substrates: various sizes of plain white envelopes

Other: acrylic paints from your chosen palette (about four colors per envelope design), small brayer, palette knife, stencils that fit along one side of the envelopes, sponge applicators for stenciling, paint pens, brush for splattering, black acrylic ink

STEP 1

Apply a dot of paint directly onto an envelope. Run a small brayer through the paint. The key to brayering is to roll and lift, roll and lift. This way the paint covers the brayer, and it spreads more evenly and effectively as you roll. Paint two or three vertical strips along the front of the envelope. I like to work in batches of about five or six envelopes of the same size, creating the same color story on each envelope in the batch. Working assembly-line style, paint this first layer, and by the time you finish, the first couple envelopes will be dry enough to start step 2.

STEP 2

Using a palette knife, scrape a different color of acrylic onto the envelope, overlapping the first color in certain spots. Finally, use the brayer again to add one more color of acrylic, as in step 1. Let the painted envelopes dry thoroughly before going on to step 3.

STEP 3

Use the brayer again to add one more color of acrylic, similarly to step 1. Let the painted envelopes dry thoroughly before going on to step 4.

STEP 4

Sponge a fourth color of paint through a stencil on to the left side of the envelope. Before you start stenciling, however, check that your envelope is the right-side up—you want the stenciling to show up to the left of your recipient's mailing address. Let this paint dry completely before moving on to step 5.

STEP 5

Using a contrasting paint pen, outline the stenciled images. I chose black because I know it will pop, and it will coordinate well with blank ink when I address the envelop or print out mailing labels.

STEP 6

Spread out as many envelopes as will fit on your work surface. Using a medium to large round brush (I used a #10), mix a bit of water into a few drops of black acrylic ink. With the brush loaded with ink, tap it over the envelopes to create random splatter all over them. Let the envelopes dry completely before filling and addressing them!

Ideas for Sharing Your Art (Joy)

- **Swap some DIY postcards:** It goes without saying that joining Hanna's DIY Postcard Swap may change your life. Hanna hosts her swap twice a year, and I haven't missed one in eleven years. It is so easy because Hanna has organized it so well. You will receive art postcards from all over the world. And last year, I met a friend who lives five miles away from me because I sent her a postcard in Hanna's swap!

- **Offer up your art:** You can follow Jana's lead and use social media to offer up your shareable art. Anyone who wants to trade art mail or receive something you've made can provide you their address in a private message.

- **Search social media hashtags:** If you search Instagram hashtags for #postcardswap, #atcswap, #atctrade, and so on, you can find posts that offer to set up trades. You can even set up your own this way.

- **The good old-fashioned pen pal:** Set up an arrangement with a friend far away, maybe someone you know in your online art community, to exchange some shareable art once a month.

- **Lift up someone who needs it:** Create a series of small postcards or ATCs and find a local hospital or nursing home that will distribute it to patients/residents.

- **Join an online art community:** I have a class on Teachable that is all about making zines. (Zines are miniature art magazines that you make to share or exchange.) I've arranged an exchange in the Facebook group for the class. You can join the class at a discounted rate just because you purchased this book! Use coupon code SYJ10 at checkout.

"Get Messy" is a wonderful art community. The focus is on art journaling, but this is another wonderful way to experiment and play with mixed media. As a member, you can join clubs within the community for trading ATCs. Check page 119 for more information on both of these options.

- **Surprise someone:** You no doubt have a whole address book (or contacts list on your phone) full of addresses of friends and family. Who among them would not want to receive some of your art in the mail? Send it!

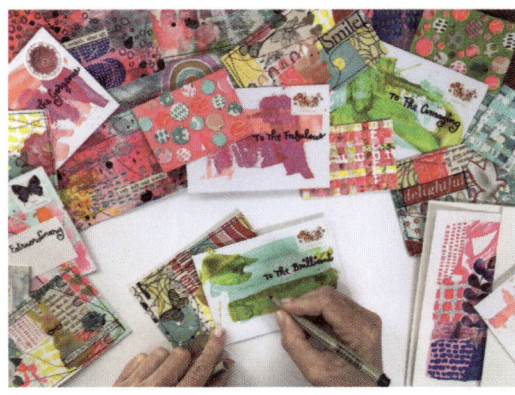

Resources

Supplies

Brands and colors of acrylic paints in my chosen color palette:
Holbein Heavy Body Luminous Opera
Holbein Heavy Body Luminous Rose
Paper Artsy Fresco Finish Dolly Mix
Holbein Heavy Body Luminous Violet
Golden SoFlat Red Violet
Liquitex Heavy Body Payne's Gray
Liquitex Soft Body Cobalt Blue Hue
Golden Heavy Body Fluorescent Blue
Lukas Viridian
DecoArt Americana Sweet Mint
Golden Heavy Body Phthalo Green
Lukas Mint
Blick Matte Celadon
Handmade Modern Satin Avocado
Golden Heavy Body Primary Yellow
Golden Heavy Body Iridescent Gold (Fine)
Golden Fluid Quinacridone/Nickel Azo Gold
Golden SoFlat Cadmium Orange
Liquitex Soft Body Naphthol Crimson
Charvin Heavy Body Caribbean Pink

General art supplies:
dickblick.com
cheapjoes.com
jerrysartarama.com

Scrapbooking papers, die-cut ephemera, stickers:
scrapbooking.com
franticstamper.com

Vintage book text and papers:
Etsy shops
jubileeflea.com

Washi tape: Etsy shops

Spray inks and dyes:
franticstamper.com
rangerink.com

Stencils: stencilgirlproducts.com
All the stencils featured in this book are from StencilGirl Products. Here is a complete list of the names for ease in locating them:
Layers of Scallop
Abstract Natural Sun
Broken Line Columns
Stone and Mortar Version 2
Thorny Stencil
Circle Rays 6
Half Moon Slant
Pressed Leaves
ATC Mixup Missigman #1 Art Marks
ATC Mixup Missigman #2 Botanical
Botanical Wildflowers
Travel Note
Fort Hill
Sea of Grapes Mini
Repetition
Butterfly Rouen Tile
Monet's Kitchen

Art Supply Wish List

Watercolors: Mijello Mission Gold watercolor set
Schmincke Akademie neon colors set
Daniel Smith Fuchsite Genuine
Dr. Ph. Martin's Radiant Concentrated
  watercolor Moss Rose
Acrylic ink: Daler-Rowney Fluorescent Pink,
  Black, Waterfall Green
Dr. Ph. Martin's Iridescent Calligraphy Colors
  Copperplate Gold
Sakura Pigma Micron pens: black, various nib
  sizes
White sulfite paper
Precut and prefolded note cards
Envelopes
**Paper punches (including corner rounding
  punch)**
Water-soluble crayons: Stabilo Woody
Caran d'Ache Neocolor II
Aifuda rubber roller brayer set
Grafix craft plastics

Community and Connection
The Share Your Joy Facebook Group
  where we can connect and even set up
  some trades and swaps: facebook.com/
  groups/5761796573915079

Juicy*S Art: juicy-s.net
This is my website where I blog and will share
  with subscribers all my art adventures and
  offerings. Subscribe to my newsletter to stay
  informed.

Juicy*S Mixed Media Art School: juicy-s-
  mixed-media-art.teachable.com
Here's where you can find my online mixed
  media art classes.

Instagram: instagram.com/juicy.s.art

Facebook: facebook.com/juicy.s.art

YouTube: youtube.com/channel/UCp_
  DjpGy57_EbTBoptMabHw

iHanna's DIY Postcard Swap: ihanna.nu/
  postcard-swap

Get Messy: getmessyart.com

Pullouts

SHARE YOUR JOY

Doodle Vocab - Glossary

This
i n t e n t i o n
JouRNaL
felongs to:

This
i n t e n t i o n
JouRNaL
felongs to:

Postcard

ARTiST TRaDiNG CaRD

Artist: _____

Date created: _____

Place: _____

No. _____ of _____

Title: _____

Email: _____

Thank you!!

with LOVE

WILL YOU

BE MINE

HAPPY

BIRTHDAY!!

CONGRATS!

NOTE:
Pull out this page and make printer copies of it so
that you have an adequate number of backs for
your postcards and ATCs!

SHARE YOUR JOY

XOXOXOXO
LOVE
YOU!
I LOVE
YOU
XOXOXOX
MINE
always
you are
LOVED
my sunshine
KISSES
forever
kiss me
CRAZY
Valentine

BE
BAE
Cherish
Adore   Love   THE ONE

Love: noun. 1. a strong feeling of affection; 2. a feeling of desire and attraction for another; verb. 1. to feel deep affection or sexual attraction for someone; 2. to really like or enjoy very much

Kiss: noun. 1. a smooch, a smack, beso, bisous; the act of two people touching lips or mouths; verb. 1. to touch or caress with the lips as a sign of love, snog, pash, make out

Passion: noun. 1. a strong and barely controllable emotion; intense physical love; 3. intense desire or enthusiasm for something

Acknowledgments

To my family: Scott, Tess, and Harry, I am so grateful for your love and support. Scott, without all your hard work supporting our family, I would not have had the flexibility to engage in the creative journey that led me here. Thank you.

To Anne: Thank you for encouraging me to enter the Walter Foster 100 Years Celebration Book Contest. You believed in me and helped me believe in myself.

To friends near and far, including my amazing art community, whose love and support have lifted me up. You helped me love myself enough to find what I love and act upon it.

To StencilGirl Products: For giving me the opportunity to create with wonderful stencils and be part of a creative team that feels like family.

To Ingrid: For showing me that Pilates can be a mindfulness practice. Your training and friendship have kept me sane and healthy through some big challenges, and I am so grateful.

To Hanna and Jana: Your participation in this book means the world to me. I so admire your generosity and authenticity and am honored that your art is part of this.

To Annika, Hailey, Liz, Lydia, and Pauline: Thank you for your guidance and patience in helping me create this book. I could not have done it without your amazing skill and talent.

About the Author

Sarah J. Gardner is a mom, a practicing lawyer, and a mixed-media artist and teacher. Starting in 2007, she began exploring mixed media as a host of Girls' ARTisan Camps for her daughter and her friends from school during the summers. She began hosting adult art workshops, which she calls Art Play Dates, at her home in 2019. In 2020, she was a guest host for Everything Art's Wanderlust, an online art journaling course, teaching six lessons that year. She has taught several other online courses, including Fodder School 1 from Willa Workshops and One BADASS Art Journal hosted by Embrace Your Art and has begun providing her own classes from her online Teachable school, Juicy*S Mixed Media Art School. She was a creative team member for StencilGirl Products from April 2021 to March 2022, and in spring 2023, she launched a series of her own stencil designs from StencilGirl Products. And of course, she's shared a lot of art!

You can find her online via the following links:

juicy-s.net

instagram.com/juicy.s.art

facebook.com/juicy.s.art

youtube.com/channel/UCp_DjpGy57_EbTBoptMabHw

juicy-s-mixed-media-art.teachable.com